ROCK *or* CLAY

Building the Foundation of Your Life on Jesus Christ

ASHLYN RICHARD

CLAY BRIDGES
P R E S S

Rock or Clay: Building the Foundation of your Life on Jesus Christ

Copyright © 2024 by Ashlyn Richard

Published by Clay Bridges Press in Houston, TX

www.ClayBridgesPress.com

Unless otherwise indicated, scripture quotations are taken from the ESV® Bible (The Holy Bible, English Standard Version®), copyright © 2001 by Crossway, a publishing ministry of Good News Publishers. Used by permission. All rights reserved.

eISBN: 978-1-68488-110-9
ISBN: 978-1-68488-109-3

Special Sales: Most Clay Bridges titles are available in special quantity discounts. Custom imprinting or excerpting can also be done to fit special needs. Contact Clay Bridges at Info@ClayBridgesPress.com

Contents

Introduction

This book has been on my heart for a couple of years, and let me tell you, I know some very talented writers who could have written this much better than I. But if writing this book has taught me anything, it's that our ability is not in us; it rests on the One who upholds us. Jesus is our Rock and our Redeemer, and our life should be built only on Him. Over the past weekend, I went on a retreat with my church's youth. I was a middle school girls' leader. In one of the sessions with all my girls in front of me, I began to pray. As I was praying for God to do work beyond my ability—which is all His work—He graciously revealed something to me.

The way Jesus chose to die was symbolic, and it was all for us. He chose the cross where He breathed His last breath so we could breathe in Him. But one thing that had never crossed my mind was the posture in which He died. He died with his arms stretched out wide. He took our sin with arms open wide, and now He welcomes us with open arms into communing and abiding with Him. He knows our sins and died for them, and still He invites us into Himself with open arms. We can bring our brokenness and our broken prayers and praises all to Him because He wants us to run to Him, knowing that His arms will not close until we are safe in those arms.

Jesus wants nothing more than His children to know His love and build their lives knowing that only His love is enough and worthy of praise. When we allow Him to speak in the silence, in the chaos, and in the good, the bad, the ugly, the beautiful, the peaceful, and the confusing, we can be quiet because we know we have built our house on the sturdy rock that won't fail when waves come. Jesus wants to build for us a foundation that won't mold or decay. Like clay, we will mold to Him, and that is all we want. We want a foundation built on praise because it is rooted in the character of Jesus. So let Him excavate you, redefine the bounds, and rebuild you to be set on the only thing that is unchanged.

Chapter 1

Address the Cracks

There are subtle cues in all our lives that are evidence of a fragile foundation. The first step is to address them, not neglect them, and truly examine what the strings of our lives are holding onto. Addressing that there is something that needs to either be fixed or completely reestablished is often the hardest part. I am someone who hates to acknowledge that anything is wrong. I would much rather feel that sting for a minute, not address it, and move on like nothing ever happened or will continue to happen. That problem is something we will be examining and addressing together throughout this book. For my avoiders out there, I urge you to not shy away from acknowledging the hurts and the shifting of your foundation, even if it was years ago. It matters, and God loved you so much that He felt your hurt and gave you the most perfect example of how to carry your human nature and human hurts of life to the Father who wants to ground you in Him.

The devil is very good at what he does. He tries to make us think that the cracks are him as he tries to shake you. While most of the time that is true, he often uses the cracks and mishaps in our life to distract us from addressing the true sinful nature in ourselves and the world we are attempting to build our lives on. When building any structure, the cues of a bad foundation don't always show up right after it is placed. It usually shows up many years later. The devil's biggest scheme when this happens is to let the problems divide, fester, and eventually cause a crack that he hopes will be big enough to break you entirely. Wouldn't it be great to recognize the problems when we are building the foundation of our lives so when we see the cracks, they won't ruin our whole house?

When you see the cracks—whether big or small—you must address them and the root of what caused them. When I was researching various foundations and how foundations are formed, I stumbled on a quote that gave me the utmost joy and hope. "A crack means things are moving, but they have not entirely broken . . . yet." This is the redemptive grace of our good God. He may let you move for a bit, but He will never let you break. You may look at a crack and think, "Wow! I am done for; I can't ever fix that." For the longest time I echoed that very phrase. And to be honest, it's true. You cannot fix anything—but God can. So as you dig into the depths of your heart, soul, life, decisions, and everything else, don't try to make your life look pretty and act like there are no cracks in it. Call the One who wrote the blueprints, and shift your focus to the beautiful masterpiece your life is intended to be and still is when you let go and let God.

Depth of the Damage

There are often two categories of cracks when it comes to structures. There are structural cracks and non-structural cracks. The construction industry explains that structural cracks are when the foundation has moved, while non-structural cracks are due to concrete shrinkage during the curing process. Looking at this through a spiritual lens, there are some things within our hearts and while walking with God that have shaped us to be who we are today. The truth of the matter is not whether there are cracks but rather how it is affecting the way we believe and live out the gospel.

Here is an example of a non-structural crack in your life. While you were learning about the Lord, loving His Word, being saturated by a godly community, and serving like crazy, the enemy whispered a subtle lie to you and skillfully planted it in your heart so you would shy away from trusting God with a certain area of your life. Even though it may not have affected you at the moment, it has now caused a crack in your life, and you are afraid to give God all of you. Your tendency now is to rely on yourself to fix the small things in your everyday life and only give Him the big things. A foundational crack is something in your life that completely shifted your view of the way you see God and your relationship with Him. It could be anything. You may have had an abusive father, so now you cannot even imagine a Father being abundant in grace and love. This thinking shakes your faith and turns it into works, not grace. It causes you to constantly work for perfection, which is unobtainable, when what God truly wants—and you truly need—is proximity to Him.

What we now need to know is what the Bible says about foundations and placing your foundation in Christ. The Bible talks about this very process in 1 Peter 5:10, which says, "And after you have suffered a little while, the God of all grace, who has called you to his eternal glory in Christ, will himself restore, confirm, strengthen, and establish you." We must know where we are being called. We must know that our hope is not on this earth but is rooted in the eternity promised us with God's immediate and everlasting grace. Once we have this Kingdom mindset, the rest of this verse will make sense. We will know that nothing good in our character comes from us; it comes from the Lord and therefore must be sustained by the Lord. It is so important to keep in mind that building your life on Christ and for Him may not be easy, but God tells us that in the end, it is more than worth it.

The first step is that God must restore us. According to dictonary.com, *restoration* is defined as repairing or renovating, to return to its original condition. What does that mean for us as Christians? The world may say we are getting better, and we naturally want to go forward, not back. But in the context of restoration, you may be thinking about returning to the faith as a child and running to God with no hesitation. While that is so good and so needed, I venture that we should take it back to the very beginning—in the garden. God wants to restore us to Himself and to the same proximity that Adam and Eve had with Him in the garden. They took their daily walks with God—actually *with* Him. God wanted to make a way for that again, so He sent His Son, Jesus. But He does not want us to wait until we get to heaven to have that same proximity with Him. He wants us to live in such a way that not a moment passes that we aren't conversing with Him. He wants to restore His children to be dependent on Him and in discussion with Him constantly, just like in the garden.

The second step is that God must confirm. That left me speechless! We can know the general meaning of something, but when we look at the purpose of each word, we see the deeper thought behind it. It not only helps us formulate an idea but allows us to see God's idea behind it. The word *confirm* means to establish the truth or correctness. It is astonishing that the God of the universe wants to establish Himself in us. He wants to establish the good, the truth, and the righteousness that He placed in us long ago. He wants to rid us of all evil and establish the image of Himself that He graciously placed on us.

The third step is that God must strengthen your foundation and you. A building is only as strong as the foundation. Let me save you a lot of time and a lot of learning. God is the strongest foundation there is. There is nothing better. He is the Alpha and the Omega. He builds, rebuilds, and sustains. Building your life on Him is not guaranteed to be easy, but it is the surest and most rooted hope that everyone longs for, and that is even more than we can grasp. The way He makes us stronger is by making us lean more on Him. It sounds a little counterintuitive, doesn't it? That's because when we are the weakest, we are actually the strongest. When we feel weak, God is the strongest in us and can show us how great and strong He is. One of the ways we are strong is by becoming more like Him.

Often we see Jesus replying in humility and with peace. People can look at this and see Jesus in the light of being afraid or timid, but it's just the opposite. He calls us to the same gentle and kind nature that He treated everyone with when He was on this earth. It took strength for Him to say as He hung on the cross, "Father, forgive them, for they know not what they do" (Luke 23:34). That took strength and accurately displayed how love and grace are often more powerful than the typical image that comes to mind when we think of the word *strength*.

In the fourth step—the curing process—God must establish us. *Establish* means to set up on a firm, permanent basis. He wants to set us up forever on Him, not dependent on anything else but Him because He is all we need. When we are called, He promises that we are affirmed and secure in Him. Some people try to justify their actions with this affirmation, but God calls us to be affirmed in Him and His ways. We are called to be the salt and the light. Our light will look foreign to the rest of the world, and it is supposed to. You may often feel that your world is shaking when all the people in your life who are not Christians seem like they have it all together.

But we are called to more. Jesus assures us that on this earth we will have trouble, but we can take heart because He overcame the world. That is what we base our lives on and why we are able to triumph instead of trip over the gains or losses that come with this life. We are not established here; we are established in eternity.

Cues of a Bad Foundation

Throughout this book, we will look at the ways Jesus lived out a firm foundation. We will also look at the ways we can fix our eyes on eternity in a way that completely shifts how we build our lives on this earth. My prayer for each of you is that your perspective changes to a building up of the body of believers, Jesus's name, and eternity. What we do matters, and every day is an opportunity. Let's not shift anymore. Let's not ignore the cracks. Let's set up our lives on God's foundation and watch in awe at what He builds.

Knowing whether your foundation is solid usually comes during a time when things are exposed for what they truly are. A blog about getting the foundation right said, "You have to start the project, clear away some of the cover-up before you realize how deep the problems go."[1] So, to my fellow avoiders, it's time—time to stop painting over

---

1 "Building on Rock: Why It's Critical to Get the Foundation Right," *J. B. Simmons*, May 29, 2018, https://www.jbsimmons.com/blog/building-on-rock-get-the-foundation-right.

the problems in your life and actually address that there is a crack that goes far deeper than you think. For some people, the root is as deep as the soil, and for others, the devil has capitalized on your tendency to overthink and has forced the crack down to the foundation of your life. Either way, both need to be addressed so the masterpiece God intended you to be is a welcoming place that ultimately leads to God's beautiful, perfect, and eternal house in heaven.

As we said before, the cracks in a foundation can be structural or non-structural. Let's first address the more severe structural cracks. If it is a structural crack in your life, the call is to immediately address it and ask God to structure your life on the right foundation—God Himself. If it is a non-structural crack, you need to ask God to remove or mend the things in your life that are prohibiting you from being the best welcoming vessel for His Spirit and His plan. What is interesting to me, however, is the cause of structural cracks. Eppconcrete, a concrete foundational company, explained the main causes of structural cracks like this: "Various things cause structural cracks, including—but not limited to—expansive soils, voids under the foundation, soil that can't properly support the structure, soil that wasn't adequately compacted before construction, and improper grading that causes water to pool near the foundation."[2]

---

2 Dave Epp, "Structural or Non-Structural? Understanding Foundation Cracks," *Epp Foundation Repair*, February 3, 2021, https://www.eppconcrete.com/structural-or-non-structural-understand-foundation-cracks/.

That means the main cause of the most poorly structured construction is soil. So we can see how crucial it is that we choose the correct soil to build our lives on. Now it's worth asking why. Why is it so important that we have a sturdy foundation for our lives apart from a well-lived life? The reason that should be of utmost importance and require our utmost attention is that we are not and should not be living just for our structure on earth. We are looking to the structure already laid for us in eternity.

If we are only living for right now, that is a sad life to be living for. We must shift our perspective to be building for eternity. With the mindset shift to eternity, we will start building our lives to look more like the heavenly structure. We are also not building it alone. We are all working together to build up a whole city for God as we keep our eyes on the celestial city. Matthew 22:37–39 echoes this sentiment. "And he said to him, 'You shall love the Lord your God with all your heart and with all your soul and with all your mind. This is the great and first commandment. And a second is like it: You shall love your neighbor as yourself.'" We are to love God first and love others. This is non-negotiable. So we should be living and building our lives on the correct soil for God, which then shows us how to live for others.

However, a key part of this passage is a verse that is not as well known, but it helps define the action and application part of these verses. Matthew 22:40 says, "On these two commandments depend all the Law and the Prophets." The very word *depend* is the basis of its meaning. *Depend* means to be controlled or determined by; to rely on. We see in Galatians 3:24, "So then, the law was our guardian until Christ came, in order that we might be justified by faith." The law is dependent and controlled by love for God and God's love for us. The law was given to us as a gift to help order our lives with love for Him and love for others. The law and the prophets built their teachings on these key principles. That means we also should build our lives on these principles.

Our daily occurrences should but often do not rely on God's wishes and His ways because our focus is not on how we can best love God and love others. Our society today praises the inward, self-oriented focus of our lives. It looks more on the interior decorating of our "house" that covers up the cracks rather than focusing on a sturdy structure. That structure shouldn't be worried about being pleasing to the human eye but being seen as a treasure through an eternal lens. Turning our lives completely around to depend on God's blueprint takes going to the base of our lives and building it up toward God. To do that means we must make sure we have the right soil and the correct foundation in place. This is a lifelong journey. Some days will be harder than others, but we must make sure to look at each action through the lens of eternity and the daily goal of loving God and loving others. We need a heart that is willing to surrender and sacrifice.

Chapter 2

God Is Wider Than
Your Wound

Telling the difference between signs of minor settling versus major damage is important—because the sooner you address structural problems, the easier it will be to repair them.

—Edens Structural Solutions[3]

My guess is that there are at least some of you who have seen the signs, thought about them, realized you didn't know how to fix them, and ignored them. I could raise my hand for some of those things in my

---

3 "Cracks in Walls or Foundations: Which Ones Are Structural Problems?" *Edens Structural Solutions*, May 13, 2021, https://edensstructural.com/cracks-in-walls-or-foundations-which-ones-are-structural-problems/.

life as well. Different parts of life can cause different types of cracks, depending on how you let the devil utilize each one. What may have started as a tiny crack has made its way up to the ceiling.

Maybe you have felt the many tasks placed on you until you cannot handle the pressure anymore, and a little burst of emotion and displays of someone who is not perfect have slipped through. Perhaps you feel like you are walking a bit funny because the floor has shifted, but you just swept it under the rug. Things look a little off, and opportunities are closing, but you feel like you must play it off like it is just a waiting season. We have to decide when we will start looking and start fighting off the seeping of the world and start ebbing off the lies for the need of perfection. We must long for the embodiment of Christ and ground ourselves in the root of His character.

Ceiling Cracks

This type of crack can run from the floor, up the wall, and all the way to the ceiling. This crack is very severe and can be caused mainly by the formulation or upkeep of the structure. A common cause is a leak or moisture damage. The greatest risk and reason it requires so much urgency is that it could cause the whole ceiling to collapse. Each home has joints that hold up the roof, and once the joints experience a weight that is too heavy to bear, they give.

The greatest and most common way we do this today

is by placing our protection in something other than the Lord's goodness. Although countless times in the Old Testament we see the Lord protecting the Israelites, and we see His physical guidance in the New Testament, and experience His personal provision in the present, we still turn to other things. It makes me laugh to remember how many times I assume I know more than God without even saying it with my words. I say it with my actions on a daily basis. We all do; it is part of human nature. However, God is faithful, and we are called to die to ourselves and trust in Him.

Although we have seen God work miracles in Scripture and in our lives, we turn from Him and look to things we know will ultimately fail us. Mark 4:19 says, "But the cares of the world and the deceitfulness of riches and the desires for other things enter in and choke the word, and it proves unfruitful." Let's examine some of the reasons we do this. We'll use the magnifying glass on the crack, look at some examples at the center of the cave-in on the ceiling, and then find where the crack stops to hopefully prevent it from going farther.

The most common reason people do not allow God to be their protection is simply that He is not physically present. I've encountered countless people who say they just need something more present. Although this theory is disproved by countless sections of Scripture, I can grasp what they are trying to convey. God is not physically here, but He is omnipresent—which means He will never leave. You cannot touch Him, but that doesn't mean He cannot touch your heart and change your life forever. In Ecclesi-astes, the writer—the preacher, as he is called—explains that he has chased after every "good thing" the world prom-ises would fulfill him, and he says emphatically that it is all vanity. But in a very interesting verse—Ecclesiastes 1:13—he explains his heart. "And I applied my heart to seek and to search out by wisdom all that is done under heaven. It is an unhappy business that God has given to the chil-dren of man to be busy with." We will examine the deep truths of this verse later, but for now, we will focus on the word *heart.*

The word *heart* in Hebrew means the center of your inner life, including your mind, will, and emotions. Once the Lord touches your inner life, your mind, will, and emotions are transformed. That is why Proverbs 4:23 says, "Keep your heart with all vigilance, for from it flow the springs of life." This was a warning foretold to the Israelites in Deuteronomy 11:16: "Take care lest your heart be deceived, and you turn aside and serve other gods and worship them."

The heart is so crucial to the affection of our lives. The writer of Ecclesiastes saw firsthand that placing all your being in the protection of the world is faulty and all vanity. How-ever, the Lord is so good and gracious to offer us the best alternative. "Trust in him at all times, O people; pour out your heart before him; God is a refuge for us" (Ps. 62:8). God offers Himself as protection, not only for our physical lives but also for our heart cries and our eternity. But we often choose to think we can only protect one of those things—not our eternal, not even our hearts, but our fleshly lives because that is what is tangible to us in the moment.

If we are truly only touched by the physical, how is God going to satisfy that? He knew from the moment He created us that we would react more to what was right in front of us, so He got right in front of us. A countless number of times I have seen girls and guys sell out and go to a person's house, not seeking intimacy for their hearts but their flesh. The saddest thing is when they try to justify it by saying, "God cannot be here physically for me, so why is it wrong to have someone else fill that role while God does the rest?" The simple answer to that question is that God fills it all.

Yes, He is not physically here, but He is a friend. He places friends, mentors, family, and many people in our lives not to be a physical coping mechanism but to be someone who points us to the intimacy that Christ offers. It quenches every physical and fleshly longing with a satisfaction in Him. Proverbs 18:24 says, "A man of many companions may come to ruin, but there is a friend who sticks closer than a brother." A brother or sister sticks by your side no matter what comes. They won't shy away from calling you into light with love. They will get the ice cream and tissues when you are hurt, and they will go throw axes with you to get the rage out. God knows we can't do this on our own, so He sends people to encourage us and keep us accountable for His way in us. That doesn't mean He gives us people as our purely physical medicine. He wants us to invite people in to be a helpful tool in working for eternity with every part of us. Although God walks with you sometimes, it is helpful to see a friendly face walking in the same way with the same end goal in mind.

Another argument against the satisfaction of having a physical presence is that we are called to not dwell or set our minds on the things of the flesh. The struggle with putting protection in something tangible is that it will ultimately wear away. Our bodies will give way to gravity, a fence will rot and wear out, our clothes will stretch or shrink, and jewelry will lose its luster and value and become tarnished. If we put our value, our protection, our refuge, and our everything in material things, they cannot and will not be able to carry the weight. For guys and girls alike, I have seen people place their identity and protection in their physical image and strength. While being good stewards of our body is important, it can easily become an idol. The Lord counters this innate sin in us by saying we should do all for His glory— which means our image is His image.

We are image-bearers, and the best way for us to be image-bearers is by heeding God's instruction. If you try to hold up that ceiling by making sure you have the biggest biceps or the most defined abs, that will give way. On the opposite side, if you glorify comfort and neglect health, you will not be able to operate at the same capacity and therefore not be the best version of yourself to be a vessel for the Lord. Romans 12:2 says, "Do not be conformed to this world, but be transformed by the renewal of your mind, that by testing you may discern what is the will of God, what is good and acceptable and perfect." We are not to focus on the physical wants of our flesh but on the will of God.

Since our heart is easily swayed by the world, we must make sure our mind, will, and emotions are stayed on God. He is the One who will hold up the walls of our lives and be our perfect protection. But first, let's address the general thought when it comes to the heart, its protection, and where it most readily gravitates.

The Lord made us have heart ties so we can be tied to Him and tied to a spouse. When a man and a woman experience physical intimacy, there is a soul and heart tie that takes place. A heart tie is something that simply makes your heart tie onto and rely on whatever you are tied to. This was divinely placed by God so we could rely on Him but also so we could develop a deep communion with our brothers and sisters in Christ.

We must make sure our mind is stayed on Christ and, most importantly, held up by Him. Jennie Allen in her incredible book *Get Out of Your Head* goes into great depth about our humanity. She explains how our minds can prohibit our advancement of the Kingdom and the gospel if we do not take captive every single thought and turn it into a thought for Him. Our mind tends to try to do a lot of things on its own. We try to rely on our intellect and wisdom when they are tainted by our humanity and our ability to only fully comprehend the present. God is all-knowing and created all. It baffles me how every time we think we know better and look at different ways to make sure our understanding is foolproof, it most definitely isn't. I'm overwhelmed with God's grace at the thought of how many times I think I know more than He does and try to outsmart Him. He quickly shows me how backward that thinking is by humbling me quickly. When we start to search for true wisdom like Solomon did, we always realize that we are not wise, and the only way to study and obtain true wisdom is to rely on the only One who knows all, simply because He made all.

There once was a girl who searched and searched to find the exact answer to her life. She spent years wrestling with even the tiniest decisions and found that God's will for her is not an exact answer. Much to her surprise, she was not heartbroken by this truth, but rather it brought her much freedom. This freedom came from her not striving after one picture of what her life should be but by a daily faithfulness to the One who reveals every good thing in His timing. That girl is me. For many years I heard people say over and over from various circles around me, "I'm just trying to figure out God's will for my life" or "I really feel like His will for me is . . . " or even "This is God's plan for me." Probably the worst to hear is "God planned for us to meet." Yes, people can even use manipulation of God's will to get you to date them. Guys, don't use that one when you're asking a girl out.

An organization for young adults called The Porch, held in Watermark Church on Tuesday nights, covered this very topic through its podcasts and sermons. David Marvin, the lead teaching pastor at the time, used the analogy of an arena. God's will is not a particular seat but a section in the arena. It may not be as clear as we all would like it to be—not a yes or a no answer—but it will align with what is shown throughout Scripture about God's character and faithfulness.

There are two parts to God's will. There is the known will and the unknown will. It is covered by His grace, and His will for us is His known will. His unknown will is the events that He knows will happen in our lives. As long as we are obedient to His known will, we will be more prepared whenever opportunities in His unknown will come about. Hearing this changed the way I view the future and how I act in the present. God is so good and shows how good He is just by laying out His will and wants for us in such a clear way as written down for us in the Bible. The examples and teachings of the Bible are His known will—His will and desire for His children. The Bible is the longest, most ravishing, best love letter we could ever receive. The best way to align the will part of your heart to rely on His protection is to read about His provision. His protection for His children is seen countless times throughout the Bible, promising on a daily basis that we will not fall as long as we are in His arms.

Let's talk about emotions—not everyone's favorite topic. I have served in the children's ministry at my church for almost seven years. There is a book on the bookshelf that the kids want to read over and over, even if they know the whole story and all the characters' names. It is called *What Am I Feeling?* by Dr. Josh and Christi Straub. It's interesting that even three-year-olds who are ruled by emotions want to learn more about them. It is often easier to let the natural emotional response to an action or event in our day-to-day lives determine our next response. It's so easy, which makes it the likely avenue to take in times of outrage, chaos, panic, or sadness. Since it is so easy, the devil uses it frequently to pull us farther from the peaceful understanding and way of the Bible. A very wise statement in this children's book says, "A feeling is just a feeling—it's not in charge of you." The simplicity of this saying is so hard to grasp in our day and age because the devil tries to say that our feelings *are* in charge of us. The devil says it's not just a feeling, and we're justified in our actions. He is of the world, so what he capitalizes on is anything that hones in on our human, sinful nature.

Feelings could be provoked by the Holy Spirit, but even if we rely solely on the emotional aspect of our faith, we miss the true gravity of what the Lord wants to reveal to us through the wisdom of his Word. He wants us to know His character, which is full of love. An example throughout our culture today is the word *love*. The Bible says that God is love. However, our society classifies love as a feeling rather than an action. The reason this is unbiblical is because love is an action—it is a choice, not a feeling. The most well-known and famous verse in the Bible is John 3:16: "For God so **loved** the world, that he **gave** his only Son, that whoever believes in him should not perish but have eternal life." It doesn't say God so loved the world that He felt a great desire for His creation, His children, and did not seek them but pondered over the overwhelming emotion toward them. A feeling should be a check engine light for your heart that provokes an inspection, paired with the diagnosis in the Scriptures.

The first person who comes to mind when I think of someone who used emotions to try to protect themselves instead of depending on the strength of the Lord was Samson. When he saw the daughter of a Philistine, he did not think about anything else because he let his emotions fog his Spirit-led wisdom and discernment. Instead, he was led by his flesh, which showed through this conversation with his mother and father. "'I saw one of the daughters of the Philistines at Timnah. Now get her for me as my wife.' But his father and mother said to him, 'Is there not a woman among the daughters of your relatives, or among all our people, that you must go to take a wife from the uncircumcised Philistines?' But Samson said to his father, 'Get her for me, for she is right in my eyes'" (Judges 14:2–3). He was blinded by her beauty and run by his feelings of lust and desire for her.

Something to notice here was how quickly this all played out. We don't know the exact amount of time between when he saw her and when he told his parents that he wanted her to be his, but I assume it was written like this to show the haste of the human flesh. Jesus in His time on earth, in bodily form, never ran or rushed into anything. The Bible only says that He set his face toward the cross since that was His mission—to take away the sins of the world. What I have found is that we often have a heavenly mission and an earthly mission.

We have an earthly agenda and a heavenly one. But something interesting is that hurrying to accomplish either one is often a contradiction to the other. That is how it is supposed to be. We have to see that the heavenly mission is something we should hyperfocus on while living at a godly pace like Jesus did while He was on earth. The saddening reality that we are all guilty of is that we often hurry to accomplish our earthly mission and are slow to fulfill the heavenly mission set for us. While Samson was hurrying with his earthly mission to find a wife, he neglected his spiritual or heavenly mission to live for Christ and use the Lord's strength that He gave him for God's glory.

> Then Samson went down with his father and mother to Timnah, and they came to the vineyards of Timnah. And behold, a young lion came toward him roaring. Then the Spirit of the Lord rushed upon him, and although he had nothing in his hand, he tore the lion in pieces as one tears a young goat. But he did not tell his father or his mother what he had done. Then he went down and talked with the woman, and she was right in Samson's eyes.
>
> —Judges 14:5–7

The parents were right here, but I digress. The reason Samson did not tell his parents was because the devil harvested Samson's emotions of anger and resentment toward his parents because they showed disdain for his "love."

Samson rushed to the woman he longed for because if he went quickly, no one could talk him out of it. If he told her of his strength, she would feel the same awe for him that he did for her, and he was fully and completely justified in his own eyes. All this secrecy came from the guidance of his emotions and desires with the lack of actual guidance or guidance by the Spirit.

When Samson held the feast for his new marriage, he told the riddle that only he knew because of what the Lord produced from the lion. His wife provoked his emotion out of her own fear that her people would burn her family's houses. Once she knew the answer to the riddle and told her people, Samson was outraged. He struck down 30 men and took their spoil. "In hot anger he went back to his father's house" (Judges 14:19). He went back to the only place that would not use emotions as judgments to their actions. His wife was given to be the wife of his best man, for she was no longer right in his eyes. Why? Samson realized he was not looking through the lens of the Spirit but of his human emotions.

After Samson was enraged and gave away his wife, he set fire to the Philistines' grains, broke through their bonds, and killed 1,000 men with the jawbone of a donkey. Through all of this he relied on the good strength of the Lord. He longed for water, and when he was searching for water, he saw himself as the Lord's servant and therefore subject to His will and protection. Samson said, "You have granted this great salvation by the hand of your servant, and shall I now die of thirst and fall into the hands of the uncircumcised?" (Judges 15:18). It's obvious through this verse that Samson did not want to die of thirst, but he recognized that all that had come about was from God's helping hand. He thought that dying was better protection than living without the strength of his Heavenly Father. But he knew that the Lord would protect him and that he could rely on Him.

Take note of what happens next. "And God split open the hollow place that is at Lehi, and water came out from it. And when he drank, his spirit returned, and he revived. Therefore the name of it was called En-hakkore; it is at Lehi to this day" (Judges 15:19). God split open "the hollow place." Some things in our lives seem empty. We don't doubt that God can do anything, but we just haven't ever been refreshed from the hollowness of areas in our lives. In order to be filled, the thing that fills you must be full. God is overflowing, and all He is looking to do is operate in the hollow places. But Samson had to call out to the Lord to fulfill his need.

Notice that when Samson drank from the water, God's Spirit returned. The act of returning is an act of getting to the simplest state in order to be enraptured by what is true and good. This is more than a feeling; it's a divine calling home. Samson felt revived. Think of a time when you did a very intense workout. You felt like you just took a shower in your sweat. You come home, take an actual shower, and get out of the hot or cold water clean, refreshed, accomplished, and just so good. This is the reviving that the Lord wants to do with your soul. He wants you to trust Him, serve Him, wrestle through things in Scripture that don't make sense, bring it all to Him, let Him wash over you with His perfect wisdom and love, and leave you with a revival of hope, purity, and encouragement to do it all again for Him.

Something else to note is what the name of the place was called. En-hakkore means "the spring of him who called." This spring would not be there had not Samson called out. So the first step to receiving God's divine protection is to call out for protection. Samson knew that only God could supply the physical and spiritual needs he so longed for. I urge you to allow God to fill the hollow spaces and trust that He will fill them with exactly what He knows will revive your spirit, which is Him. He will keep your ceiling from falling because the crack is filled with His Spirit, and what flows from it will be profitable for many as it ripples out from your life.

Now let's look at the story that most people know about Samson. It's the story of Delilah. Delilah asked Samson three times, and three times he told her a lie for he had not told anyone. The fourth time, she asked from the perspective of the heart. "How can you say, 'I love you,' when your heart is not with me?" (Judges 16:15). After she vexed him to the point of telling with all his heart, he gave in to the protection and resilience of her heart's wants instead of God's good desires of protection. If you don't know how the rest of the story goes, here's a quick summary. Samson's head gets shaved, the Philistines capture him, they gouge out his eyes, and Samson prays to God to give him strength. At a party of 3,000 Philistines, Samson breaks two pillars that hold the whole building and dies with the Philistines after God grants him His strength once more.

When God was upholding Samson, the pillars of his life were the power of the Lord. With the Lord he was strong; without Him he died to the very thing he thought his emotions longed for. Samson was constantly infatuated with Philistine women, and his emotions drove his love life. The rest of his life, however, relied primarily on the Lord's strength. When finally his emotions got the best of him, he turned to full reliance on the pillars that were cracked and not strong. Notice also the difference in reaction and feeling after relying on his human emotional love versus the strong love of the Lord. Samson was weak, hurt, angered, and annoyed, and ultimately it led to death. But God is so good that when He upheld Samson, he was strong, was revived, had peace, and was able to navigate between the emotional response and the wise response to the various temptations that came his way. God is so good that even when all of Samson's strength was taken from him, God had a gracious plan for redemption and hope. "But the hair of his head began to grow again after it had been shaved" (Judges 16:22). God constantly longs to grow you in your weakness and make you stronger in His strength and provision. In the end, the strength that killed the Philistines and brought justice was not Samson's but the Lord's. Samson had to physically die and also die to the protection he had placed in his emotions and other loves. He had to put God at the highest place in his life and trust Him in whatever he allowed under his roof.

Let's look now at David, a man after God's own heart. To be honest, I struggled with this. David murdered Uriah, coveted, and committed adultery. But as I have learned more and more, even though David messed up, he always went running back into God's loving arms because he trusted God with all his life. David knew and had learned about God's character. He knew that although sin separated him, God's grace was great. I think the beautiful thing about David is that we are like him—Christians who are truly trying to live out the gospel, seek Him, fail, and then seek God again and fail again. Yet God still chooses us. He could have chosen any other person to be in the lineage, but He chose David because He wanted the picture of the Christian walk to be one of constantly seeking and relying on the Heavenly Father as David did. David sought God with his mind, will, and emotions. David was a man after God's own heart, so God gave David His heart so he could be transformed into His likeness.

Jeremiah 29:11 says, "For I know the plans I have for you, declares the Lord, plans for welfare and not for evil, to give you a future and a hope." Many people are worried about what their future looks like and worried less about seeking God with their whole hearts. The verse before that encourages us not to worry about that. "I will fulfill to you my promise and bring you back to this place" (Judges 29:10). If God knows the plans, we do not have to know them. Sometimes it would be nice to plan around certain things, but that means we would be in control or stressing over the things we ultimately cannot control.

God does not show us His plans out of protective love for His children. The only thing He wants our minds focused on is following Him and seeking to know Him, not just His plans. By knowing His faithfulness in the past, we are able to more fully trust that His loyalty and faithfulness to us will be sure in the future. Jeremiah 29:13 is God's call-to-action statement to His loving notion to trust Him: "You will seek me and find me, when you seek me with all your heart." When we seek Him with all our hearts, we are sure to find protection because we find Him. We see less of the issues and more of the solution. That does not mean every little thing in our life will feel completely stable. It means that every little thing won't matter when we put it next to the overall firm grasp that God has over us and our eternity. It also is a sure thing. God says we will find Him when we seek Him with our whole heart.

My word for the year last year was *wholehearted*. The year before that it was *surrender*. It's funny how God works like that. I can tell you for sure that I am not perfect at wholehearted surrender by any means, but I did learn a lot about surrendering my situations and then surrendering my heart to Jesus. The year I felt challenged about surrendering to God, I had to surrender a relationship in my life that I was trying to hold onto. God is so good that even when He called me to surrender and I couldn't, He surrendered it for me—for my good. The next year I felt the call to focus on being wholehearted. In hindsight, I now see that He was simply preparing a stepstool for me to ultimately give all my life to

Him. I had to learn the hard way that you have to not only surrender the things you are holding onto in your life but also surrender your whole heart. People talk about being saved and often accompany it with this saying: "I accepted Jesus into my heart." Although yes, the entering of the Holy Spirit is an action that takes place during this moment, I would argue that you are actually giving Jesus your heart and letting Him do with it what He will. People say, "I gave my life to Christ" and then continue their testimony. However, giving your life to Christ is a daily occurrence. It calls for waking up every morning and saying, "Lord, I decided a long time ago (or a short time ago) that my life is an offering for You, so let me be Your hands and feet today; my life is Yours." He is our breath, so every breath should be directed toward Him. But this wholehearted surrender every day has to be taken day by day, step by step, and moment by moment to reorient our hearts—the mind, will, and emotions—toward Him. It is the surrender of our strength and then resting in His perfect presence and stability.

My friend, instead of just a word for the year, choose a phrase such as "just for today." That means you are saying, "God, I don't know what tomorrow will hold, and yesterday is gone, but I will choose to be faithful to You today because You are faithful to me always." I challenge you to say that prayer every day for a week, from the moment you wake up until you go to sleep at night. I encourage you to see your mind, will, and emotions change into a heart of seeking God, resting assured that if you seek Him with your whole heart, you will find Him. He will reveal Himself to you, which is all you need to be faithful in that day.

Something that sometimes worries me is my finances. Pursuing a career in ministry does not always guarantee a large earthly paycheck. I'm certain that the reward of hearing my Savior say, "Well done, good and faithful servant" is plenty reward and more than I could ever ask for or deserve. Seeing people come to know the amazing King who brings life where there once was death is also priceless and worth more than anything money could buy. However, as much as I am satisfied with this, society is not. My living situation as a woman is not always as certain as my family or I would like it to be. But there is a verse that always gives me comfort that the house the Lord has built for me is more than enough for me and all I need. "And my God will supply every need of yours according to his riches in glory in Christ Jesus" (Phil 4:19). Recently, with this verse in mind, I prayed this prayer: "Lord if it would make me a better vessel for your gospel and better in any way in expanding your Kingdom, I want it. Have your way in me. If not, if it is only out of my fleshly desire or worldly pursuit, close every door possible for me in obtaining it."

This life was given to us by Christ so our every effort should be to give it back to Him. God has proclaimed throughout Scripture that the best time spent on this earth is in servitude to bring more people to know His good name. If there is anything of our wants that we are structuring our life around that does not ultimately point to the house of the Lord and eternity, it will cause cracks and will not leave you operating at full capacity for the Kingdom. We may not notice it in this life, but we will in eternity. The best prayer to be praying now is to be available and willing with all your heart to the advancement of His Kingdom. That means knowing and trusting that the place you are in figuratively and locationally, as well as the things in your life, are exactly what God needs for you at this moment in order to be the best vessel for His Kingdom. We should also pray that God will close and open the doors needed for us to wholeheartedly surrender everything to Him and for Him.

Chapter 3

God Is Wider Than
Your Wound – Part 2

Diagonal and Stairstep Cracks

Diagonal cracks often appear at the tops of doors. Stairstep cracks appear anywhere diagonally across walls. The result of these cracks is that the whole wall starts to slant. The biblical application of this is that we all have been affected by the culture in some way or another. I'm sure you've heard the saying, "We all drank the Kool-Aid." John 17:11 says, "And I am no longer in the world, and I am coming to you. Holy Father, keep them in your name, which you have given me, that they may be one, even as we are one." We are in the world but not to be of it. However, as we can see with the differing views of each generation, the culture we live in affects at least some ways that we approach or view things. The ultimate light we live in should be the ever-burning lamp of the Lord, but we don't always use that light to guide us. We rely more on the dim light of the world that ultimately turns into darkness.

If you haven't noticed already, the world is very dark. When it gets really dark, we constantly fill ourselves with its darkness. Before you get hopeless, just know that if you have filled yourself with the depravity or despair of the world, the Lord is the best night light out there and can relight your life with His hope and goodness. Isaiah 42:16 says, "And I will lead the blind in a way that they do not know, in paths that they have not known I will guide them. I will turn the darkness before them into light, the rough places into level ground. These are the things I do, and I do not forsake them." God can be the opening to His window of light instead of our being halted by the slanted and jaded doorway of the world and its cynicism.

Certain members of my family love the news. They like being caught up with current events and knowing the various arguments being made for particular political points of view. There is nothing wrong with that, but I would rather know the basis of what's going on and see what the Lord— not fallen humans—say about it. There is a fine line between being in the know and it being all you know. I think the biblical thing to do is learn the sides being argued and check that reasoning with the Bible.

However, the tendency is to know too much about the world and not enough about the world to come. Eternity is what truly matters, and as soon as we take our gaze off that and put it on the problems of the world rather than the solution and what we are fighting for, our view shifts. It is not all of a sudden that we are unable to see the good, but over time as we fill our minds with the problems of the world, we lose sight of the solution of heaven. That is often why we see people who have lived through a lot become jaded and cynical. They have seen and lived through the corruption of the world and people from all over, and it has become so overwhelming and in need of a fix that they give up trying to see the good.

Hear me when I say this. I am not saying that we should try to sugarcoat life and pretend that everything is okay. It is actually just the opposite. I argue that we should see the hurts and depravity of our world, which immediately causes us to look to the Lord's overwhelming goodness and place our hope in that. An elderly friend of mine was a very spunky, fiery lady. One day when I visited her, I asked if a lot of people came to visit her in the home for the elderly where she lived. She very honestly said to me, "Nope. All my friends died." As sad as this was, she did not deny the truth of it. She was aware of the reality of what was going to happen. I hurt for her, but I'm so glad she said it. As I left her, I realized that I need to appreciate the time I have with my friends. I need to cherish them and never take for granted the precious and lively moments I have with them.

Pastors are often very aware of the brokenness of the world. My pastor, in particular, does a very good job of addressing it anytime something major comes up in current events. He takes it head on and makes sure to show the congregation what God has to say about that particular issue. He does that because we are in the culture but not of it. What happens around us affects us; we cannot deny that. But it cannot define us. When we let it define us and the actions we take in life, it transforms our views to despair instead of hope. How is that helpful to non-Christians who don't know the same hope we have? It not only affects our witness but also our spiritual journey, our relationship with God, and our urgency, willingness, and availability to obey the Lord's calling.

Something that also shows the structural damage of the stairstep and diagonal cracks is noticing that the windows and doors won't open. Imagine with me that you are in your house. You plan to make a delicious, moist, rich chocolate cake. You get distracted and leave it in the oven too long. You smell something off with the cake and suddenly see the dark silhouette of the cake in the oven. You finally open the oven and take it out. You realize that you forgot to set the timer. When you opened the oven door, a huge cloud of black smoke protruded and overtook the entire kitchen. It became very hard to see in the once-lit kitchen since the smoke was clouding your vision. You finally reach the window you were once trying to find and open, but you see that the crack you neglected to fix above the window frame has now bolted the window shut. You try to go out the door but find that it won't open either. You are stuck, and your only option to breathe in clean air is to go into a room that is equally as dark but far enough away from the smoke you can still smell. Although this is a very dramatic story, it accurately describes what could happen to our hearts if we let the darkness and slanted view of the world close the doors that the Lord wants us to walk through and become blindfolded to the light and hope the Lord wants to show us.

As the slanted cracks continue to protrude from your wall, you can see that there are often wide gaps along the door and window frames that are prohibiting the door from opening. As we lean into the depravity of the world rather than the saving grace of the Father, we tend to look more at the gap that is expanding than the functionality of the hinges. Since we are so used to seeing the bad in the world, we can easily become consumed with the growing darkness within us to the point where we become pessimistic and no longer have the child-like faith and hope that God so desperately wants for us. Since we are looking too deep into the wound, we often are not able to look at the crack or the gap for what it truly is from a bird's eye point of view.

If we were able to truly remove ourselves from the slanted view and dark view of the world, we would be able to see that the slant we have given into has shifted and jammed in the hinges, which won't open the door. The devil doesn't want you to open the window for the Lord's fresh wind and rejuvenation. He also does not want you to walk through doors of opportunities so you can share the joy of the Lord. So if you are someone who finds it very easy to see the bad in the world or the worst-case scenario rather than the good in any situation, I encourage you to earnestly petition the Lord to help you step back, see the crack, slant for what it is on your life, and pull open the window to let His light in to truly refresh your soul. The only way you can do this is by addressing the crack, looking to the only One who can mend it, and focus on Him more than the daunting damage.

The structural implication of this crack is that it often is a result of settling and structural damage. Maybe you got used to bad things happening to you, and so at some point in your early childhood you gave up hoping for good because you thought you were unable, unlovable, or undeserving of such goodness. You got so used to it that you settled into a constant state of complacency and disappointment. If this is you, I am truly sorry and want to speak this over you right now before we get into anything else. God loves you and has amazing things for you.

You may not be able to see them at the moment or even on this earth, but know that we are not of this world, and we are not to stay in this world. Your eternal safety, joy, and reward are in heaven. There will be no settling in eternity, and every dream will be fulfilled because it will be perfected in Jesus. I also charge you to stop looking for your joy and future on earth but rather seek the One who will never fail you or be faulty. Jesus recognized and even felt the same sensation of not having His hopes come to be. Jesus prayed in Matthew 26:39, "And going a little farther he fell on his face and prayed, saying, 'My Father, if it be possible, let this cup pass from me; nevertheless, not as I will, but as you will.'"

He hoped He would not have to save the world through this means. Jesus's hope was deferred, or we would still be striving to be perfect by following the Old Testament law.

God recognizes that hope—whether heavenly or earthly—that does not come to be and diminishes the spirits of the one who hoped for it. Proverbs 13:12 says, "Hope deferred makes the heart sick, but a desire fulfilled is a tree of life." God has assured us that if we believe and hope in Him, He will make all things right again. Even though the world makes it very hard to hope, we have assured hope because it was given to us the moment we chose to trust in Jesus. Asking for hope in God is not a bogus prayer. David tells us to petition with our hearts to hope in Him again since He is our salvation (Ps. 42:5). Romans 5:5 says that "hope does not put us to shame, because God's love has been poured into our hearts through the Holy Spirit who has been given to us." What good news that is! We have hope instilled into us. A heavenly love was placed into us, and therefore out of love come joy and hope—heavenly joy and hope that will never be put to shame since it is eternal. Ephesians 3:17 says, "So that Christ may dwell in your hearts through faith—that you, being rooted and grounded in love." How incredible is it that God would not only instill His love in us but then root and ground us in it so we have something firm to hope in— something that will certainly not move with the whims of the world but with the steady hand of the Father who we rest on and are comforted by.

The Bible describes Jesus as both a lion and a lamb. He

was slain yet reigns victoriously. He is firm and steady yet gentle and comforting. If you throw all your cares on Him and put your hopes in His hand, I promise you that He will be gentle and do things you never would have envisioned for yourself. Even if you can't see the beauty in what you thought was wasted hope, God promises that the hope is not wasted but will be redeemed for Him and to Him. Psalm 130:7 says, "O Israel, hope in the Lord! For with the Lord there is steadfast love, and with him is plentiful redemption." The redemption may not be immediate or be what you thought it should look like on this earth, and it may not even be on this earth. But God has promised that redemption will come, and in Him it will be full. In Him is complete fullness, more than we could ever hope for.

During a night of worship with my worship team at an event called Lead, my dear friend took us through a time of spiritual introspection called inner heart healing. I completely thought I had nothing I was holding onto as worldly wishes. Had I thought wrong! She started by asking us to think of a time when we felt truly hurt. She said to put ourselves in that atmosphere and see what we were thinking and feeling at that moment. I was taken back to a place where I did not think I was being hurt. But as certain situations cleared over time, as conversations were clarified, and through individual growth, I saw that the moment I was taken back to was, in fact, a true time of hurt. The numerous tissues on the table should have been clue enough that that moment was hard, to say the least.

As I was taken back to that painful moment, my friend said to look around the room and see where Jesus was. At the time I was there, I thought God was the farthest away, and I did not see any light at the end of the tunnel. But when I remembered and looked around the room, in my mind's eye I saw Jesus, not at the other end of the room but right next to me with His hand on my shoulder saying, "It is okay, daughter. I'm right here. I know you are hurting. I'll never leave you nor forsake you. I see you." I'll pause right there to acknowledge that God said He saw me when I couldn't see Him anywhere. He said He loved me and would continue chasing after me when I couldn't see any way that He would make amends. He called me worthy of being chased after, even when I was not chasing after Him, and I found myself slanted by the dark situation around me. Jesus sees you and is the way out. Even though we often find ourselves leaning more toward the negative or the hurt that is right in front of us, Jesus says He will change all our hearts to bend toward Him instead of the world if we seek Him and ask Him to step in.

Okay, now back to the inner heart healing. As I felt Jesus, saw Him, and sought out what He wanted to make of my remembrance of that hurtful time, my dear mentor and friend said to take that hurt and hold it out in my hands. She said to see what God makes of it. As she said that, the hurt was turned into soil. The soil looked dirty and dead to me at the time. But then she said to give it to God and see what He gives back in return. As I reluctantly gave my hurt soil to

God, I cried and cried and cried—not a single tear or a cute type of cry, but an ugly sob. But my tears turned into tears of joy very quickly as I saw what Jesus gave me back—a flower. As I saw this flower in my hand with Jesus holding my hand as I held it, my friend said, "Maybe He gave you . . . a flower." And that's how I knew it was divine intervention—what my friend calls a God wink. She then led us to give back to the Lord what He had given us and see what He does with it. As I gave the flower back to Him, I saw myself dancing in a field with that very flower in my hair.

Looking back at that dark moment made me realize the deep hurt I felt and the deep sorrow I saw in myself. I never thought that girl sitting in Starbucks crying her eyes out would be dancing in a field with nothing but smiles and the sun shining on her as she looked at her Father with the most fulfilled joy imaginable. What we see is often not what God sees in us. We see the moment by moment and can only fixate on the darkness. But God looks at us with loving eyes, the way He looks at His Son, Jesus. He looks at us through the lens of the most perfect Heavenly Father and sees us only as His beautiful son or daughter.

Maybe the way you should view the world is as the Father says you should—through the lens of eternity, knowing this is not your home. But maybe the jaded view you have is a self-view. During a conference for an organization called Sparrow, the head director made the distinction between image and identity. That common misconception is what traps so many people into thinking they cannot fully be themselves because no one would like the real them. Let's be honest. That statement is the saving grace and need for Jesus.

Without Jesus we would be hard to love. We wouldn't need a Savior if we could love perfectly and if we didn't get run down emotionally and physically. We need to rely on Jesus's grace and goodness to fix our mess and turn it into a display of His strength in our weakness. But often we capitalize on our weakness and either sit in our hurt and mess or try to fix it ourselves. Ultimately, we cannot do that and fall back into the crack of self-condemnation and deprivation. That leaves us hopeless and stuck, prohibiting us from walking through open doors and closing them from the Lord and from sharing His gospel.

My prayer for you as we go through this book together on this heavenly journey is that we will not be the ones to close the doors or windows. I pray that we will be open in our hearts, which includes our minds, will, and emotions, to what doors and windows the Lord wants open and which ones He wants closed. We should not be the ones to close opportunities that God possibly wants for us, putting us back in control when we just borrow control. We are not bearers of it; we just behold it. The façade of control that we think we possess is given to us by the world, but I argue that it is much better to place all control in the One who has it all. We are merely stewards of God's giftings. Do not limit His hand by limiting your own.

God sees you not just as you are but as you have been and as you will be, and He still calls you beloved. You have a purpose and a God-given purpose. Focus on God, and turn your hesitancy into gratitude and willingness to see His might in you. Let God show you the beauty of who has made you and what He has made you to be as His perfect daughter or perfect son. He wants to show you this. He wants to show you Himself. Once you get a glimpse of His goodness, you will not want to dwell or fixate on the slanted darkness that once bound you. As it says in Matthew 11:30, "For my yoke is easy, and my burden is light." His yoke is good and right, and it will set you free with the freedom to serve Him to your fullest. And that is where real, full joy is found.

Chapter 4
Horizontal Cracks

These are the most problematic type of crack you may find in your home because they result from water damage. The cause is usually poor drainage, which leads to moisture getting into your walls and weakening them. This problem will only grow worse and put your home at great risk. If you see horizontal cracks anywhere in your house, call the experts for an immediate assessment.

—Edens Structural

L et's call Jesus immediately because He is an architect, a mender, a sustainer, and a beautifier. He planned, placed, and prepared you for where you are at this very moment, but He cannot grow you if you do not let Him. He gave us free will, but His true desire is that we freely come to Him with all we have and with all we are. God sometimes leads us through storms, but the question is not if we make it out of them but how Jesus offers His hand to guide us through it. All we have to do is take it. A common misconception is that if we take Jesus's hand to lead us through, our journey will be easier. But this is simply not true. The storm can sometimes leave a scar from a harsh blow, but instead of giving that scar to God to show His might and His glory, we harvest it for ourselves and hide it away for fear that if anyone sees it, they will think of us as less or damaged.

The easy thing to do is to tap out and not address the various hurts within. As we saw in the previous chapter, fixating on all the bad can keep us from serving God and building our lives on His purpose and plan for us. On the flip side, if we don't address the hurts inside, the rain from the stormy season can seep into all areas of our life and eventually affect our connection with the soil. If you have built your house on clay soil, the clay will expand when it comes in contact with water, thus causing hydrostatic pressure that causes the structural foundation beams to crack, bend, and bow. This expansion could be because we decided to do the quick fix to the hurt, or we might have allowed the pressure to build up until finally the beams cracked. That leaves us wondering and hurt because we never established a drainage system.

As I looked up the various issues that occur when water seeps into soil, I was absolutely shocked by what came up in my search. Here is the question I asked: How do you fix water seeping under the foundation? The answer by SAS Home Services said, "If you see water dribbling into the basement through cracks or gaps around plumbing pipes, you can plug the openings yourself using hydraulic cement or polyurethane caulk. This is a simple do-it-yourself job that typically costs less than $20." To the average human, that sounds like a pretty sweet deal, but that does not fix the root of the problem. Yes, it may stop the crack from getting bigger, but what will happen when another crack pops up? Eventually, you will get tired of filling in the cracks. You might just let them be or try to get to the root of the issue. As a loving sister in Christ, I say in the kindest way possible, don't settle for the quick and supposedly easy fix. It does not work and will leave you more broken than how you found yourself in the first place.

The fix for the crack promises that it is a "simple do-it-yourself job" and that it "costs less than $20." The walk of salvation is not simple and is not a simple do-it-yourself job. It is long, hard, and full of trials, but it is worth it. You also cannot do it alone. Even Jesus had disciples so He could model for us what doing life with others looks like. It's them loving you and you loving them, no matter what they are facing. It's you being part of a body of believers in a church or ministry that is passionate about building each other up and caring for one another as they go through the life they are living for Him.

Being a person who does not like to allow others in, I can understand people who would rather take on all the problems of the world and simply bear them. I sympathize with those who understand that it is easy to take on problems and hard to give them up, even though we should. There is some sort of mental block in letting it all go to God because you feel like you should be able to fix it all and that you are handling it. Let me be a kind sister at this moment. You are not handling it, but God wants to and will as long as you acknowledge this. If you are anything like me, you hate being a burden to others. That's partly because you have once been burdened by others and would hate to do that to someone else—although you would never put it in those words. You allow people to place burdens on you because you want to be needed, and you want others to want you around because you are known as kind, helpful, wise, and caring. And that's how you want to be perceived. The problem with this is that you are the drainage system for their storms. You have no way to let out the water; instead, you are letting it fester and fill up inside of you. That causes you to feel drained because everything that was once functioning is overflowing with baggage and hurt. That is all on top of the water in your system that has been filling up all the while with everyone else's hurts you have been taking on.

But God—those two words are my lifelong security because when everything within and around me feels like it is cracking under the pressure and being swept away by the depravity of my humanity, I can rest in the consistency of the good God who holds it all together. Because He holds it all together—including me—I do not have to. The verse I constantly remind myself of is Matthew 11:28: "Come to me, all who labor and are heavy laden, and I will give you rest." Sometimes I have to physically place myself on my knees to stop my heart, mind, and body from racing. Then I take all my worries off my shoulders, put them in my hands, and give them to God. I physically put them in Jesus's hands.

This is hard to do when trust has been broken in the past. You feel so weighed down that you cannot even examine where it started to seep into your foundation and when you started to crack. The best thing is that none of that matters. All that matters is how you plan to stop letting things seep into your foundation and how you will drain the hurts and pain from yourself and others. There is no step-by-step way; it is purely just by resting on the saving grace of Jesus. We have to put ourselves in the light that He is the Savior and that everyone needs saving. The key thing to remember is that He is still a Savior. He did not just save you once; He saves you every day! He not only protects you but cares for you. And what about the things you think are too small—the things you should be able to bear without their affecting you too much? Yup! He wants to save you from those things too. He loves you. That does not mean you will never be bogged down with worries again, but the hope now is that you know what to do with them and who is best equipped to hold them. It is not you—it is Jesus.

A story in Genesis shocked me with its practical implications to our everyday lives. In Genesis 33, Jacob is on a journey back to his father's land. He is making his way to Succoth and Shechem. On his way, Jacob sees his brother Esau coming up the road. Yes, this is the brother he stole the birthright from. But as Esau met Jacob, he embraced him and kissed him, for he loved his brother who had wrestled with God (see Gen. 32). Esau is overjoyed by Jacob's company, for the Lord was with Jacob and had blessed him. Then Esau offers to lead them along at the pace Esau was going, with his men leading.

> Then Esau said, "Let us journey on our way, and I will go ahead of you." But Jacob said to him, "My lord knows that the children are frail and that the nursing flocks and herds are a care to me. If they are driven hard for one day, all the flocks will die. Let my lord pass on ahead of his servant, and I will lead on slowly, at the pace of the livestock that are ahead of me and at the pace of the children, until I come to my lord in Seir." So Esau said, "Let me leave with you some of the people who are with me." But he said, "What need is there? Let me find favor in the sight of my lord." So Esau returned that day on his way to Seir. But Jacob journeyed to Succoth, and built himself a house and made booths for his livestock. Therefore the name of the place is called Succoth.
>
> —Gen. 33:12–17

Jacob could have looked at Esau, even though he got the birthright and blessings from the Lord and envied the state Esau was in and the pace he was going. But something that caused Jacob to look at the situation objectively was the words God had said to him that he held fast in his heart. He knew God was with him and called him on his way back to his father's house. He also knew what was given to him—his family. God had entrusted him with a blessing, and although it may not have looked successful to the rest of the world because of the long journey he seemed to be endlessly on, Jacob knew it was worth it and that it was divine.

Often we find ourselves in this struggle to see our brothers and sisters in Christ walk alongside us, and then slowly but surely they pass alongside us. The temptation there is to long to be moving at the pace they are moving. But God— those two words are sovereign, powerful, and peaceful. God reigns, and He is the point. Therefore, it's His wants, His way, His will, and His wonder. He has you exactly where He wants you.

My mind automatically goes to the story of the tortoise and the hare. In this classic story, the hare was moving at a faster pace than the turtle, but the hare got cocky, got sidetracked, took a nap, and ultimately lost the race. The hare lost the race because the tortoise knew his way. The tortoise was not taken by every little thing that caught his eye; he simply kept with the path and the pace he knew could sustain him. Comparison will cause a similar thing to happen to you. It will make you look at the hare that is zooming past you, seemingly looking like they have it all together—the race in the bag so to speak. In this situation, there are three ways you could respond. Try to keep up with their pace, stop running completely, or take it one step at a time.

The problem with keeping up with the pace of the person

you are looking to be like is that God does not want you to run their race. He wants you to run your race. He did not equip you with the things you need to run someone else's race. He equipped you to run your race. Let me paint a picture for you. Let's say you and your friend decide to go for an adventurous weekend getaway. However, your friend made a mistake in the message and typed cliff diving instead of rock climbing. You show up with a backpack full of swimsuits, sunscreen, and a list of great cliffs near the area. Your friend shows up with a backpack full of chalk, climbing gear, and maps of various routes near rocks. You would not try to climb these rocks without the right shoes, and your friend would not want to attempt to cliff dive without a bathing suit. This example is an exaggeration, but it shows you that God does not want you to attempt to climb the rocks in your bathing suit only to fall and seriously hurt yourself in the process. He loves you too much to let you do that to yourself. He prepared a way for you so you can walk in it, knowing that if He calls us to dive deeper into Him and stay in one area instead of climbing up in the world, then that is exactly where we want to be. In God's arms, in His will, and walking in His way, at His pace is the best place you could ever be. His will is for you to trust Him, believe in Him, and follow Him with everything you have. Knowing Him is truly all you need to know.

If you are a future-oriented person, you will spend a lot of energy simply trying to figure out the next steps. Speaking from experience, it is taxing, anxiety-inducing, and honestly depressing to constantly try to control every circumstance in front of you. The pressure buildup, which we will address later, keeps building until ultimately we burst. We burst because we were not built to hold that type of weight. God can and does hold that weight if you release control back to Him where it belongs. But the question still stands. How do we do this? It is not a one-and-done process. It is daily surrender, recognizing that this life is not our own and that whatever we do should be done in His strength and for His Kingdom. That change of mindset, however, is not even ours to fix or control. It all is in the hands of the Lord.

As I look back at myself over the years, the best advice I tell myself is to take in God's refreshing breath and look up. Breathe in the fresh air of His truth, love, and presence within you, and let Him decide what you do with that breath. Trying to figure out His plan is not His call for us. He wants us to constantly move closer to Him and figure out His character. Finding Jesus is finding where we need to be. And here's the best thing about that. Finding Jesus is not hard to do because He promises that He is with us. He promises that He will never leave us. He makes Himself easy to find. What He puts in our hands is what we do with Him once we find Him.

Let's say someone gave you a beautiful piece of blown glass that fits perfectly in the décor of your home. They planned exactly where you would put it and how it would look. You greatly appreciate the gift. You would not smash it on the ground or hide it away. The hope is that you will put it in the center of the room to bring it life. It will be a conversation starter for all who spend time at your house. That is what God does. He gives us the gift of salvation, a beautiful and intricate masterpiece. But it is ultimately up to our discretion for where to place it in our life. He wants us to place it in the center because no matter what the area around it looks like, it will be seen as beautiful, simply by its majesty and captivating presence.

In the long run, do not worry about where everything will be placed or how everything will occur. Just worry about where you place the masterpiece—called the gospel in your life. Focus on it, thank the Creator, and never hide it away because it lights up your entire room and brings an indescribable peace. Take the beauty of God's rest in your hands, and let God do the rest. My challenge is that you pray this prayer every day for the next week before you go to bed and allow the peace that surpasses understanding to transform your heart, soul, and mind to the goodness of God and His sovereignty over every inch of your being. Let this prayer be your soul's honest cry to the Lord with no reservations and nothing withheld. Fully surrender to Him who longs to carry you and all the things you've been holding onto.

Resting on God – Valley of Visions

O God most high, most glorious,
The thought of Thine infinite serenity cheers me,
For I am toiling and moiling, troubled
and distressed.
But Thou art forever at perfect peace; Thy designs
cause Thee no fear or care of unfulfillment.
They stand fast as the eternal hills.
Thy power knows no bond,
Thy goodness no stint.
Thou bringest order out of confusion,
And my defeats are Thy victories.
The Lord God omnipotent reigneth.
I come to Thee as a sinner with cares and sorrows,
To leave every concern entirely to Thee,
Every sin calling for Christ's precious blood.
Revive deep spirituality in my heart.
Let me live near the Great Shepherd,
Hear His voice, know its tones, follow its calls.
Keep me from deception by causing me
to abide in the truth,
From harm by helping me to walk in
the power of the Spirit.
Give me intenser faith in the eternal verities,
Burning into me by experience the things I know.
Let me never be ashamed of the truth of the gospel,
That I may bear its reproach,

Vindicate it,
See Jesus as its essence,
Know in it the power of the Spirit.
Lord, help me, for I am often lukewarm and chill;
unbelief mars my confidence,
Sin makes me forget Thee.
Let the weeds that grow in my soul be
cut at their roots;
Grant me to know that I truly live only
when I live to Thee,
That all else is trifling.
Thy presence alone can make me holy,
devout, strong, and happy.
Abide in me, gracious God.

Chapter 5

God Won't Give You More Than You Can Handle

The soft foundation—Soft foundation material that can become displaced by the structure.[4]

When people look at the daunting reality that comes with following Jesus and laying down their lives to project His, they start to buckle under the pressure of what that notion brings. However, we are not the ones in charge, and therefore, we cannot take on anything that He does not give us. Christians are to live out and be the hands and feet of Jesus. That pressure is not on us

---

4 *National Engineering Handbook*, "Part 646 Construction Inspection," *United States Department of Agriculture*, July 2012, https://www.irrigationtoolbox.com/WebPages/NEH.html.

though. God promises to prune us to be better image-bear-ers of Him, so we need not fear. Sanctification is a lifelong process, and we are merely the clay that He is turning into His masterpiece. But the fear of many is that we will not be able to carry any weight placed on us by the world or God that seems too heavy. That is the result of having a soft foun-dation, which we will address in this chapter. So get ready to have your faith and trust tested. As I am writing this, my trust in the Lord is being tested. And that is exactly what we are to long for because through testing and trials we see how sure our foundation is.

For most foundation sites, the soil in the foundation must be monitored and managed by setting up a drainage route. The water must flow away from the house, and there should be no standing water or a drought in the soil. Standing water or stress that is not addressed can cause other things to seep in and never drain out, causing your foundation to be soft and not able to withstand much else. The owner of the house probably mistakenly believes that the house can take on all the water that pours onto it without draining it in any way.

In this current self-care, do-it-yourself age, everyone and everything can be found in a constant state of go. This state of go continues until eventually everything has built up so much that it floods into every area of an individual's life. When that happens, it is easy for someone to feel washed away by a roar of emotions and feel overwhelmed by the tasks that have now left them waterlogged. But God does not want His children to live that way. The Bible shows God's faithfulness and hand in the steps of all His children, guiding them even when they disobey Him. God has promised and ordained each day. That means that if you are still breathing, you still have a purpose. Even if each day feels like the biggest battle to get through, God has already conquered, won, and placed you exactly where He wants you.

Most people are scared and try to figure it out. They become blinded by looking at the big picture for their lives. All God asks you to do is to be faithful with each moment. Something the Bible teaches time and time again is that as long as you are chasing after God and loving Him with your whole being, you are in His will. God knows every decision you have made, as well as the decisions you are making currently and will make. Let me make this easy for you. I am going to tell you God's specific will for your life. "Give thanks in all circumstances; for this is the will of God in Christ Jesus for you" (1 Thess. 5:18).

Yes, that's it. Give thanks, and give Him your all. He is not shocked by the decision you made this morning, and He is not worried that it will affect His plan. His plan and will for you is to love Him with your whole heart. And out of that love, give thanks. No matter what comes in the world, all we need to be concerned with is what will come in eternity. God promises in Scripture that all creation will sing His praise and "at the name of Jesus every knee should bow, in heaven and on earth and under the earth" (Phil. 2:10). God longs only for you to be His and that He is the object of your thanks. He often puts us through circumstances to teach us that very thing. He is a good Father and wants to kindly point us back to Him. Sometimes the kindest thing God can do is place us in the valley. But He wants you to know that if He places you there, it's for a reason. He is with you, and He will be the One to pull you out.

Imagine with me that you are hiking up rolling hills. There are clear skies, and nothing seems to be going wrong. All of a sudden it starts to rain, and you keep on trekking. At the top, you accidentally step in a puddle and don't notice the mud caked on the bottom of your shoes. You keep going until all of a sudden, the mud that has been caked on for a while causes you to slip and slide down to the bottom of the hill. You brush off the dirt at the bottom, take a deep breath, and start climbing back up. You soon find that the hill is too slippery, and at every attempt to go up, you almost immediately get pushed back down until all of you is covered in mud and despair, and you are afraid you will never make it to the top where you imagined yourself being.

This story has two ways it could go. One of them leads the person to the top, and the other one may provide more character. Let's address the first one.

The first person tried and tried, and in their exhaustion gave up. After sulking for a while, they soon realized that they had a neighboring friend who might have a rope to get them up. They called the friend multiple times, and the friend did not answer. The person never gave up calling their friend, and finally one day they picked up. The person expressed how they wanted the friend to go through their journey and did not want to disrupt their learning process. When the person asked for assistance and the friend saw it was best to lend a hand, they grabbed a rope and helped pull the person up. The person climbed the steep hill with the mud still caked on the bottom of their shoes. But as they climbed higher, the mud began to fall off as the rain poured harder on them. The person made it to the top and eventually got where they wanted to go but with much more appreciation now after what they had been through.

The other person called someone, and that person came right away to come to help them. The person had been at the top of the hill but decided to slide down the hill and walk every step at the bottom with their friend. They walked every day together with the mud slowly coming off their shoes as the rain trickled down on them every day. They sang a joyful noise together for they knew that soon the mud would be grass. The warm, cold, dreary, beautiful days came, but with every step and every song, the hopes of the person and the friend rose because they were able to see the valley as beautiful, even if it was not where they had pictured themselves walking.

Both of these people did not want to be in the valley at first and did not know where they would end up after being in the valley. Still, each found out that the valley was where they needed to be for a time to see the beauty of where they were, not situationally but spiritually. Consecration to the Lord is far more important to God than your comfort. Notice something in both of these stories. Both people never stopped calling for their friend, even if they didn't answer at first or how they wanted. The sad reality is that sometimes people have to stay walking through the valley in this life and only see the mountaintop in heaven. But whether the people were in the valley or the mountaintop, each still sought the Lord daily and fervently, knowing and trusting that their friend would be there, not to get them out but to simply be with them. They did not trust in the valley or even fixate on the valley. They trusted and fixated on their friend. That is all God wants. He wants you to focus on His sovereignty over the situation, not the situation that feels suffocating.

The friend in each story answered exactly at the right time and in the right way. The friend knew what the person could handle and what they needed to learn. If you were about to touch a hot pan without an oven mitt, your friend would hopefully warn you. But if you had just been talking about how nothing hot can burn you, my guess is that your friend might want you to learn a lesson so you would stop bragging. However, it would not make sense if your friend let you jump out of an airplane without a parachute to let you learn the lesson that you cannot fly. God will not let you fall and especially will not let you fall into something that will not make you a better vessel for Him. Sometimes the hard correction is more caring than taking the easy way out and never learning how to do hard things. Following Jesus is not easy, but it is worth it.

My grandmother always gets asked this question by one of her unbelieving friends: "Why do you believe?" Take a moment and truly think about how you would respond to that question. Why do you believe? Actress and preacher Sadie Robertson always asks a similar question: "What do you believe Him for?" My grandmother who is so wise says it gives her comfort to know she does not have to do it all on her own, knowing that she is living life for a purpose and with a purpose. Living a purpose can be hard when your purpose tends to follow the guidelines of the world's priorities. You see priorities build up and change with the season, but the purpose is constant, singular, and consistent when it's held in God's hands. God should be our priority. He is our purpose, and He will set what we need to prioritize.

My high school AP Environment Science teacher provided me with a good example. He had a purpose mindset over his tithe while he was in the valley.

When our daughter was one, my wife was mostly at home and had a part-time job at our church. At my previous school, it was becoming very clear that I needed to leave, but we weren't sure where I should go. A friend of mine was teaching at the Collin County campus at Coram Deo Academy (CDA), and she mentioned that the Flower Mound Campus needed a chemistry teacher. The job was only going to be part-time and clearly wouldn't pay enough to support our family. My wife had applied to several districts but hadn't received any responses yet. I needed to give CDA a definite answer before we had any guarantees that my wife would secure a full-time job. We prayed about it together and knew that God was asking us to take a step of faith out onto what was, at the time, an unknown. So in July 2017, I officially quit my job in Plano and took the job at CDA. Two to three weeks later (quite close to the start of the school year), my wife received an offer for Hebron HS, and we knew that God had made the unknown a solid ground. Then in 2019 (your sophomore year), I had the opportunity to go full-time at CDA. At no time during the four years in which we were living off essentially one or one and a half paychecks (beginning when our daughter was born in the summer of 2015) did we ever stop tithing. Yes, that money would have prevented us from constantly drawing on our savings, but we knew that God had called us to be faithful in our giving. And in the end, He was faithful to sustain and provide during those times.

To my teacher, that time felt as if God was allowing them to sit in the downpour of their stress, but they never stopped praying and asking for the Lord to work. But the most important part is that even though they couldn't see it, they trusted that God was working. They never stopped tithing, even when it seemed foolish to the rest of the world. It was a no-brainer to them because they knew God was over their situations and finances. After all, He was first over their lives.

Chapter 6
A House Divided Will Fall

And if a house is divided against itself, that house will not be able to stand.

—Mark 3:25

Differential Settlement Foundation

Have you ever had *"the* conversation" with a significant other? During the courtship period, it is for the most part pretty clear where the trajectory of the relationship is going, based on a multitude of things—frequency of dates, longevity of time spent together, people involved in the knowledge of the relationship, and overall joy in spending time together. All of these things are telltale signs of how the relationship is going.

"The conversation" often starts with these frightening words: "Hey! I think we need to talk" or "Hey! Can we go to dinner? I want to talk." When the guy is initiating this conversation, it usually means one of two things. Either he

is proposing, or he wants to terminate the relationship. Let's say the girl wants to assume the best so she goes into this conversation with hopes high, all dressed up, fingernails painted, and fully expecting to prepare an engagement party at her soon-to-be-maid-of-honor's house. We all know what happens next in the opening scene of the Hallmark movie with the wrong guy. The picture painted next is the girl with eyes that are gleaming and full of love toward the "guy of her dreams" that all of a sudden fades as he delivers these words from across the table: "I think we should break up."

This heart-wrenching moment is followed by large amounts of healing that need to be administered with tissues, an army of her best girlfriends, and tubs of ice cream. But the sadder reality is when that is someone's life. The wide-eyed girl's expectations were not met because she thought the relationship was going one way when all along the guy had a completely opposite idea and wanted the relationship to go in a different direction. When this happens in life, we cannot fix the different directions of our foundation with ice cream and tissues. It takes a complete rebuilding of a foundation. It's true when Isaiah 55:9 says, "For as the heavens are higher than the earth, so are my ways higher than your ways and my thoughts than your thoughts."

God wants to build our life on a different soil than what our flesh desires. Even though we know His ways are better, the temptation lies in the control of our own ways and our desire to see the fruition of our own earthly plans. The problem is with the direction and properties of the soil.

God's soil has good bearing capacity and is directed upward, unlike our soil that has poor bearing capacity and is directed horizontally.

Compressibility of Soils

When your house is built on different soils of different lithological characteristics, the house will be divided, and one part of the house will start to sink into the ground. When this happens, you can do a multitude of things. The most common response is to ignore that side of the house. Some will only use one side of the house, forgetting fully that some part of the soil is still fragile and more of the house could still be built on it unknowingly. Avoidance is not the solution because it will still be there no matter where you go, even if you decide to not put pressure on it. The house is still not whole and will never be because the whole house is not resting on the whole firm foundation that can withstand the pressure of souls, everyday life, and hardships. The main difference when it comes to the soil is the measure of compressibility of the soil. God's direction and soil are highly compressible because it has a bearing capacity that is far more than anything you can fathom on this earth.

When your house is resting on anything, it cannot withstand the daily pressures of life. One of those pressures is the daily struggle to abide in Christ. We cannot abide in Christ if we are resting on the soil of the world. Resting on the soil of your own strength cannot even compare with the strength of the Lord. The exhausting matter is the notion that you have to hold up your life by yourself and with your own strength. After realizing this, people often go to the next thing besides themselves that the world advertises as easily accessible. Yes, things may be accessible, but they are definitely not sustainable. The reason all those things will not sustain anything that rests on it is simply that it's not God. It was not created to have anything rest on it. The only thing everything can rest on is God.

We search for rest, but how often do we rest things on things that will not hold anything, things that cause us to struggle to pull them up as the thing we value is sinking? I think we do this subconsciously because we want to be in control. My Old Testament professor explained to me that the root sin, displayed in the garden, is the human desire to be our own god. We long for power, and even if we do not seek overall power and holistic control, we desire to feel competent in some regard. However, the most freeing thing is that God made us dependent and purposely not able to hold things together. We cannot hold things together because we did not create them, and we did not give them to ourselves. Even the difficult things were given to us by God so everything could be given back to Him in the end. The difficult or hard things in life will not always miraculously get better overnight if you give them to God, but now the heavy things are resting on something that can hold them up. He wants to hold you up. This freedom is the best when all support is in Him because He wants to carry you. He wants everyone to rest fully on Him because we will no longer be striving to pull up the weight of the things we are resting on. We will be simply resting—striving only to hold up God as the highest in our lives, love, and affection. Abiding in Him allows you to follow His direction of rest that continues His direction upward toward the Father and not down and away from His stability.

Drying of Soil Surface Layer

Another part of the differential settlement is the drying of the surface. I once was given an orchid to try to regrow from the stem. I was determined to regrow this beautiful plant, but as time progressed, I found that keeping up with the food and water regimen was disheartening when growth was not as fast or evident as I had hoped. That is the same thing I have found when building and caring for the foundation of life. Often we are very diligent in building a foundation for Christ. But over time, if there is no evidence of the carefully kept foundation we thought there would be or that we even perceived, we stop clearing debris and caring for its health.

One day I thought the orchid was done growing since I had forgotten to water it for a week. I figured it was not worth keeping it alive. Initially, I thought it was dead and had no potential for regrowth, but actually, it could have grown through diligence and with time. But then the stems turned dry and white with no potential for regrowth. I have perceived that the real reason foundations crack and shift is due to the unseen growth that comes from continually caring for your foundation.

Before each sports season, the coach often goes through a week of practices that prioritize the specialization and growth of the fundamentals. The purpose of this is so the refreshing of the fundamentals provides a building block for the rest of the skills to be learned that season. If someone had bad form and the coach ignored it and proceeded to teach them an advanced skill, the play would not be executed well, and the skill would not be able to be carried out to its utmost potential. The coach does this every season so players are reminded of the key things they need and know how to do. This refresher is necessary, and that is why it is done each season. This preparation never changes because even though the team or individual will face new challenges every season, the fundamental things they have built their athletic career on will never change. The tactics against each opponent will change, but the way they approach each challenge will not change with their core values. Keeping up with the foundations of your faith is thus crucial for the new and often daily challenges the world throws at you. Not caring for and remembering your foundation can cause the tools of your foundation to grow dry and dormant. Not using them will not prove to be useful since the things you built your faith on are not easily remembered and thus not easily put into practice.

Often athletes use a basic skill so much so that the skill becomes ingrained in their innermost being and thus is incorporated into everything they do. With practice, they will find how each movement or advanced skill is an advanced variation of the basic skill. Without the key principles of the move, the move could not be made. It's the same with the principles of God's character that we are supposed to build our lives on. If you believe you are loved and build your life on the love of Christ, you will show His love because you will find your comfort and identity in it. You will show His love and utilize the key principle in everything you do.

Just like how I did not water my orchid, we often forget to water the fruit of the Spirit in our lives. To produce the fruit of the Spirit, we have to be in tune and know the Spirit. To know the Spirit is different from realizing the Spirit and how He is working in your life. Actress and preacher Sadie Robertson once said, "You may know something, but to realize it will change your life." Realizing something is to make it so evident that you cannot help but acknowledge it and believe it with your whole heart. We have to re-realize the awe-striking wonder of our God. Realizing His work in the past often aids in seeing how God is moving right now. I think if we realize the power and sovereignty of the Lord, we will allow Him to move in the ways He wants to in our lives right now.

Often, we are our own problem by limiting the power and areas the Spirit can reach. We have such an earthly per-spective that what we see as impossible is an impeccable place for God to work in and renew our ground for a fresh foundational look at who He is. We forget to let the Spirit

move because often we blow past the parts that look too difficult or think they are too simple and that we should be able
to figure them out. However, at one point in all our lives, we
were only dependent. As infants, we could not even hold up
our own heads. The most we could do was breathe, and even
with that, we were dependent on God to give us oxygen. If
this was the case, why do we think we are independent with
time to "grow"?

Many say that in order to have a child-like faith, this
faith has to mature. But our dependence on Him needs to
be what we operate out of for everything in life. We give
everything to Him and base everything on Him. Trusting
Him for everything is evidence that you trust His character
and try to base your actions on that. Once we realize the cra-
ziness of some of the Old Testament stories and how God
did out-of-this-world feats, it will alter the ability we give
to God in our own lives. Realizing that the God of the Old
Testament is the God of the New Testament and the God
of your life will change how you view His power and sovereignty over everything. I surveyed some of the closest people
in my life regarding their favorite stories of the Old Testament that make them simply stand in awe of the Lord. My
cousin and my best friend both had insights and different
perspectives of the stories that simply reading it would not
warrant. My cousin loved the story of Noah and the ark, and
my best friend loved the story of Job.

Noah had incomprehensible faith. He led his family to
build a massive boat that seemed crazy to everyone except

God. This story has so many hidden gems in it that are testaments to just how amazing God is, but the part that stood out to my cousin was the fact that all the animals showed up at the ark at the exact appointed time, and in pairs.

> They and every beast according to its kind, and all the livestock according to their kinds, and every creeping thing that creeps on the earth, according to its kind, and every bird, according to its kind, every winged creature. They went into the ark with Noah, two and two of all flesh in which there was the breath of life. And those that entered, male and female of all flesh, went in as God has commanded him. And the Lord shut him in.
>
> —Gen. 7:14–16

God did not leave any kind of animal out of the renewal of the world. That not only shows how much He cares for His creation but how much He cares for the differences and diversity that help all life. It is like the care and need for the different parts of the body. The arm cannot hear, and the ear cannot link up with others around them. God cares for the little differences in all His creation that bring completion when the day is done, and He receives all the glory for our efforts. He cares for the beast and the lilies of the field.

> And why are you anxious about clothing? Consider the lilies of the field, how they grow: they neither

toil nor spin, yet I tell you, even Solomon in all his glory was not arrayed like one of these. But if God so clothes the grass of the field, which today is alive and tomorrow is thrown into the oven, will he not much more clothe you, O you of little faith?

—Matt. 6:28–30

God cares so much for what He creates. How unlike God are we? We make cookies and appreciate how good they are, and when there are too many left, we despise them for being in the house. We quickly gorge on them so we do not eat them later. We are such fickle people. As I am writing this chapter, it is Christmastime. This season for most of the world is secretly called greed fest. However, when it's Christmas morning for a six-year-old and "Santa" blesses them with the most perfect present they have been dreaming about, they are ecstatic. Sometimes they even rub it in their parents' faces, saying that Santa knows them and loves them more since he paid attention to their list. As the parents chuckle and watch their kid revel in pure joy, the rest of the day they are quickly disheartened when they find the toy on the floor next to the fireplace as their child complains and whines about what their cousin got. We are people who know good things and yet forget to cherish them.

My cousin who noticed this is also a very talented artist. She often creates something unbelievably beautiful, but then a few years later when she has progressed in her skill, she strongly dislikes the work she created years ago. While this is natural and human, it is not true of God. God stays the same and is always perfect. He does not create things that are better than other things. To praise something or someone is not reflective of just them; it is reflective of the cause for praise. If people go to a choir performance and clap at the finale, they are not only praising the individual members of the choir but also praising their talent, dedication to the music, and who gave them their talent. Whether they realize it or not, they are praising and thanking God. That simply means that the source matters and is the true thing worthy of praise.

Coffee syrup that's used to make a fun-flavored coffee is overpowering by itself, but when it is mixed with what it was intended for, it creates an array of flavor profiles that are pleasing to your taste buds. The syrup is created for something else. We are the syrup to God's coffee. We are to show others the beautiful character of God by highlighting His greatness. Thus, when people taste the coffee, they praise the creator of the syrup. If people just tasted the syrup, they would not praise the creator because the facilitator served it wrong. Often we serve ourselves wrong by presenting ourselves as worthy of praise apart from the Father. When we do this, our self-esteem is crushed because by ourselves we are not worthy of praise. But in accompaniment with the Father, we are more than loved and seen through the lens of His eyes. Thus, anything created in Him is beautiful and cared for fully by Him. My prayer for you is that you will step out in freedom, knowing that God wants you on the boat. He is your pair. He created you, walked with you through the stormy clouds, and calls you loved every day. Don't let the clouds of fear keep you from rising above the waves and gazing at His face.

When researching this story, I found facts for the mathematical timing and age that would put Noah at 600 years old when the flood came. His oldest son, Japheth, would have been 100 years old, and his second son, Shem, would have been 98. This is crazy that the sons were all in the same place and not prohibiting their father due to his age and their age from being able to physically to help. The common conception of the story is that while Noah is old, his sons are not, so they could have helped. However, this is not the case. None of them were in their prime, but God was. God was going to make all things new by using His ways that seemed ancient but were the only ones that were full of life—His life, as the text says.

Some of the species that migrate in groups are the snow goose, the pronghorn, the Canada goose, and the hummingbird. But there is no other account in the history of the world where all groups of migrating animals migrate to one location at the same time—much less the animals that do not migrate and do not fly. This means that all the animals that were not native to that region, Mesopotamia, would have had to travel in advance, which could only be prompted by an amazing and miraculous God.

Treat Your Trials

My prayer daily is that I can see God in everything and see the specific things He is trying to show me about His attributes without my perspective getting in the way. As I was going on a hunting trip with my father, I prayed and prayed that I would see a deer and be able to shoot it early so I could chill in the camp for the rest of the trip. If you have ever been hunting, you know it is hit or miss. It is so peaceful for the first two hours, but then you grow impatient and want something to happen so much that the leaf the wind moves suddenly looks like a deer eating corn. The first night as I was sitting in the tree stand, wishing for something to come up—really anything at this point—I used the silence to talk to God. I started praying and heard the call that this was a chance to spend time with my father—yes, my earthly father but more importantly my Heavenly Father.

I prayed the rest of the time, and as I was asking questions about Scripture and God's character, specifically about wants and desires, I felt as though in different ways than in the past He wanted good things, and He wanted to grant me the things I wanted for myself. As I was thanking Him for wanting to give me good things such as Himself, I felt as though He was saying to be patient and just wait and see what He will do tomorrow morning. As I left, slightly confused, I trusted and believed for tomorrow, not focusing on what He could do but on what He had already done in his Word.

The next day when we went out, I was watching for deer. I heard the call to listen to the Lord instead of listening for the small sounds deer would make. Then I relaxed and watched the sunrise. Not even two minutes later, my dad tapped me and motioned for me to look. One by one, seven deer came out of the brush. I was amazed as I struggled to get my rifle in position. I took a shot and missed. I was devastated and disappointed in myself. However, I contemplated later the words the Lord had spoken, and I recounted that I prayed to see and shoot a deer. He allowed me to do just that. He graciously blessed me to see not just one but seven deer and shoot at one. He never said I would shoot one and kill it. I also thought back to when my earthly father first asked me to go deer hunting with him. My heart had dropped because I could not even think about killing Bambi's mom. The devil is the one who steals, kills, and destroys. It is not God. He allowed me to shoot at a deer and graciously allowed me to miss it so I did not kill His beautiful creation. The point of that drawn-out story is that sometimes God allows us to see and accomplish His plan that aligns with part of ours but does not necessarily go exactly how we thought it would.

My best friend's awe-striking story that she is constantly amazed by is the story of Job. The part of the story that baffled my friend is the strength Job was able to obtain from the Lord. I think Job did not envision his life going that way. He did not envision losing all his children and his house, getting diseases, and having his friends and wife belittle him. However, he listened more to the voice of God and His strength rather than the voices and hardships that he made smaller than the voice of God. We must, like Job, make the voice of God louder so we can watch His sunrise and see later the fruit of waiting—so we can see His guidance more than the strength of our own eyes. Job did not let the details of how his life started to play out distance him from the strength he knew he had in God. God knew He could use Job to show His strength and give Job a way to treat his trials.

Treating our trials with God's strength and how Jesus treated His trials during His time on earth is our end goal. However, we can often use our eyes and ears to listen to how we think the trials should look. One particular trial I faced revisited me in a letter. At the time of the trial, all I could wish for was in this letter that showed up two and a half years later when I did not look for it or expect it. The reconciliation that was in the letter was what God longed to give me but knew I did not need to hear it until He reconciled it within me before trusting outside reconciliation. We need to look at our trials through the lens of God's strength. He will uphold us. All we need is to trust Him and know that although it may look different than what we envision, it is so much better than we could ever write for ourselves.

The Proximity of Trees with Large Roots

Willow trees are a perfect example of a large tree that requires a lot of water at its roots. My neighbor has a beautiful willow tree outside their fence near the sidewalk. Its leaves are always green, and it always seems to be healthy. Most likely it will be there a long while. However, one time it seemed extra-large was the summer my neighbors decided to put in a pool. If you know anything about willow trees, you know that their roots seek out the nearest body of water and consume it. My neighbors thought that since the tree was not directly in their backyard, it would not affect their pool. Oh, boy! Were they wrong! The willow tree's roots seemed to grow bigger that summer. They started to grow into their backyard and eventually encroached on their pool. Because of this tree, they did not keep the pool for long. The tree is still healthy and contained outside their fence.

You might be wondering what this has to do with anything. Well, it's actually what is happening all around us; we just have to open our eyes to see it. The world is the tree that is trying to soak up all the water and encroach on the gospel in such a way that all the moisture is soaked up. Any body of water that was once pure is now destroyed by the consuming power of the enemy. But just as my neighbors got rid of their pool, there are ways for us to be filled with the holy water of the Spirit and not be drained by the ways of the world.

When there is moisture in a house's foundation next to a willow tree and the moisture leaves the foundation, the foundation can shift and cause differential settlement. That is why it is crucial to know what you plant and what is being planted in or near your house. Some things need not be planted. The ways of the world had better not take root anywhere near your house. Don't water the things that seem harmless now but are not necessarily helpful. Water the words of life from the Father that only come when you are planted in Him by His streams.

Even though the willow tree is beautiful on the outside, it has a character that hides things. No one would suspect that the roots were gradually growing into the base of a home. It wouldn't be obvious partially because the leaves are so beautiful and hide all the ground but mainly because the roots are buried so far beneath the ground that no one suspects it. Its roots can damage a foundation because they take a path of least resistance—the loosest soil. It's much like the beautiful Amur maple tree that is vibrant in color but known as the most invasive species. That is what the devil does; he makes everything look beautiful on the outside but doesn't lift the leaves and show you his tricks that will rob you of your life— not just your life but the most important life, your eternal life.

Differential Settlement Foundation

Differential foundation consolidation, causing cracking in the earth fill or concrete structure or breaking of the bond between the foundation and the structure.[5]

—United States Department of Agriculture

---

5 *National Engineering Handbook*, "Part 646, Construction Inspection," *United States Department of Agriculture*, July 2012, https://www.irrigationtoolbox.com/WebPages/NEH.html.

The biggest thing that stood out to me in this statement is how this type of settlement resulted in the breaking of the bond. It can be seen countless times throughout history, certainly right now and also countless times in the Bible, how the devil often gets you to settle and let complacency set in, slowly breaking the bond between you and your Savior. Settling for what seems easy is what the devil wants—to ease you away from the comfort of the Lord, which is eternal hope.

Hope does not put us to shame, because God's love has been poured into our hearts through the Holy Spirit who has been given to us.

—Rom. 5:5

The hope the devil advertises keeps us entangled in the world, but the hope of the Lord keeps us tethered to truth, love, and grace. The devil tries to twist the definition of *tethered* to sound like a punishment. He tries to convince us that in the world is true comfort. However, its definition is supposed to bring freedom. The word *entangle* means to become twisted together with or caught in. The definition of *tether* as a noun is the utmost length to which someone can go in action; the utmost extent or limit of ability or resources. The definition as a verb is to fasten or confine with. The devil will try to convince you that the limits God sets for you are restricting and punishing; however, it's just the opposite. It grants you grace, hope, and freedom. What the devil doesn't tell us is that the world is what traps and twists everyone into a pit that is not filled with any direction of grace or hope and most certainly does not offer freedom but rather entanglement. But being bonded and tethered to the Lord brings hope that does not put us to shame because it is not rooted in the here and now.

Hope is something that is weirdly most evident when there is nothing to be hopeful about. That can be seen through the wise words of my dear friend who said, "I want a fire, but fires don't last forever." We were talking about how the general "church talk" is a fresh fire, but she was praying over this phrase for her spiritual life and asking God for a fire when He reminded her of the image of a fire and the embers turning to ash. Hope is an eternal flame because it is not based on a single encounter. It is harvested through daily surrender and trust in the Lord, no matter the circumstances surrounding you.

Paul wrote some of his most encouraging letters to the churches he had visited while he was in a prison cell. Why did he do that? It was because he was so bound to Christ and hope. He constantly reminded his flesh of the eternal hope that one day his soul would be united with Christ. Tim Tebow—author, speaker, and former football player— explained in a speech about running the race for Christ that the word *passion* in Greek means to suffer.

A person I was deeply touched by was my high school choir teacher, Sharon Miller. She had scleroderma for the last seven months of her life, and yet she still lived with the hope of eternity. She was able to do that because she was tethered to the Lord and His call for her life—to love Him and love others. Even when she was suffering, she hoped and cared for others to know the joy she had every day. She lived life well and was overjoyed at the thought of being with her Savior. Her life was anchored in things that would not drift. She lived and suffered well so people would come to know Christ. She had a hope that outlived her and bleeds into everyone she touched because God touched people through her. That hope did not come from believing the lies from the hardship but from trusting in God and taking Him at his word. That came by first knowing His Word and seeing how He has given hope to the hopeless. Consolidating His love is nothing we can do because it reaches far and wide in our lives. We just have to open our eyes to see it. Open eyes occur through a constant hope that is infallible and rooted in the joy that the foundation of spending eternity with Christ presents to all who love and trust Him.

The parable of the seeds falling on fertile ground talks about the depth to which the seed is allowed to grow. What is compelling is the key idea that sanctification takes patience. A key feature for any seed to grow is that it has to be watered. Often I try to speed up the process of being bound to Christ because the binding takes endurance and sometimes stints of pouring rain or dry heat. But each season has a purpose. Hope cannot be wasted when it is tethered to eternity.

Chapter 7
Rock: The Who

Sandstone is a sedimentary rock that is highly resist-ant to weathering.[6]

—The Weathering Module

I recently felt called to re-read parts of this book to bring hope to the *how*. The original plan I had for the rest of the book was to talk about various other signs of a bad foundation and then explain how to build a strong foundation on Christ. I bargained with God to let me put it in because so many other things could contribute to a shaky foundation. However, I felt called to let Him speak into the things already mentioned and reveal specifically to those who need the exact words that are much better than my own.

---

6 "Welcome to the Weathering Module," *Paradise Valley Community College*, n.d., https://www2.paradisevalley.edu/~douglass/v_trips/wxing/introduction.html.

We are now aware of the areas the devil could be trying to take root, and we know how to address those areas. So I think it's time to start excavating and building our lives on the firm foundation of Christ and see how the Scriptures lay out for us exactly how to do that. One of those ways is the title of this book: *Rock or Clay*. I talked to my friend's mom who has had dreams to simply live out the Hebrew word *hineni*, which means no limits, no distractions, here I am. I love this word. One of my mentors remarked how she lives without mold. That opened my eyes to the reality that for some there needs to be room for the Lord to shake up their security. Others need to be planted right where God has them and right in the firm structure He has built for them. Thus there is a need for rock in the northern parts of the United States and clay in the southern parts. But for all of us, I think the same principle applies—the way the foundation is to be prepared is with care, intentionality, patience, and dedication.

Before we get into laying your foundation on Christ, I think it is crucial to note what a construction help site says. "With dry stone masonry, gravity, friction, and the skill of the worker are what holds your stonework together."[7] God is holding you together. The skill of God is not lost in our shortcomings and pressure from the weather. The One who formed us will ultimately hold our form in Him and like Him. I have to remind myself of this often. Christ is not lost.

---

7 "Building a Stone Foundation," *This Cob House*, 2013, https://www. thiscobhouse.com/building-a-stone-foundation/.

God is not confused about what is happening in the world and to you. He formed you and will continue to form you to stay molded to His likeness. The reason it's uncomfortable is because the form He has for us is not the form the world likes to put us in.

The first crucial part of a foundation is site preparation. The first step is to "clear a level pad for your building. Make it at least 3 feet bigger than the size of your building on all sides so that you have room to maneuver about the site."[8] This may be the hardest part. The clearing away takes a deep examination. Mason King, a pastor at the Village Church, preached a sermon about awakening to courage. He talked about the societal misconceptions of what the gospel actually says and that what we believe is shaped by our growing numbness to sin since we are surrounded by it. He said, "I'm not coming for your TV; I'm coming for your consciousness." He cautioned the body of Christ to not fall prey to the trappings of the devil since he can lull your heart to sleep. We often overcome temptation and then after a little bit think we can overcome the temptation to not fall into it in the same way we once were enslaved to it.

These temptations do not have to be large, but little by little the devil uses them to try to lull you into their trappings and keep you from being fully awake to the heart of God's calling for your life. I once had an unhealthy view of

---

8 "Building a Stone Foundation," *This Cob House*, 2013, https://www.thiscobhouse.com/building-a-stone-foundation/.

relationships and did not look to the Bible or biblical books for wisdom but rather found *The Bachelor* or *The Bachelo-rette* TV shows more entertaining. But the Lord has grown and sanctified that part of my heart. However, I recently started watching the latest season since I wanted a new show. I thought since it had been years since I watched it religiously every week it would not affect me in the same way—leaving me feeling lonely and disgusted by the fate of this world. Although I knew the truth and did not start watching it for the previous reasons, I soon was reminded of the emptiness that flooded my earlier years. Recognizing this, silly as it might be, was a way to acknowledge my brokenness and my dependence on God to reign over my humanity.

Purging from anything is never fun, but it is fulfilling. Much like after an extended fasting period such as Lent or the first month of the year, we will see that all we truly need is God's sustaining Word and life. But purging even the things that could have been a previous blinder to seeing His glory could bring more life than expected. Taking time to dedicate all you do in your everyday life to honoring the Lord for His glory with holiness will take time and effort, but in the end, it will show that God wants you to not take life too seriously but to take Him and His kingdom seriously. To most people, that sounds like I am saying you should devote everything and thus do everything with so much holiness that you become a nun. No, do not think this is what I am suggesting. I am simply saying that you should know yourself, know God, and know what propels you to increase His name or tempts you to elevate your own. So leave room for Jesus (for all your life). If you need to, make room for Him.

The next step in preparing the site for your foundation is setting up batter boards. "These allow you to run string lines for the outside and inside of your foundation trench. Always use a line level to level these strings."[9] These batter boards are a godly community you can trust. They are the friends the Bible describes as sticking closer than a brother (Prov. 18:24). Developing those friendships allows them to be your barriers. We are called to be the light in the darkness; however, one candlelight by itself cannot light up a whole community or country on its own. That is why God puts people in our lives so we can be lights together. This barrier also helps if one friend steps into a very dark place and tries to bring light but eventually gets blown out. The friend whose candle is still burning can relight their wick. The key, however, is friends who keep each other level.

There is a saying that goes like this: Life is all about balance. That is very true in many ways. But there is a lie the devil tells us in that. The lie is that we have to keep it all balanced. This is not true because God is the One who keeps us level and balanced in Him. One of the ways He does that is by putting people in our lives who can help keep us grounded in the truth that remains level.

I have been very blessed with some of the best friends in

---

9 "Building a Stone Foundation," *This Cob House*, 2013, https://www.thiscobhouse.com/building-a-stone-foundation/.

the whole world, but I'm slightly biased. My built-in sisters and I have been friends for close to seven years and hope we will all be sisters for life, no matter how far away we are from each other. But to those who do not have this yet, I want to assure you that we were not sisters overnight. It took time, and I also want to assure you that although it was not effortless, it did feel natural. So for the person longing for this sort of companionship, know that it is out there and will come, but it takes a little bit of time. To the other person who has been trying to force friendships left and right or trying to make something work and it feels strenuous, I encourage you to pray and see if that is the friendship God has for you. My friends and I have definitely had our moments that were not great, but for the most part, we all have been encouraging, uplifting, and real with each other.

The main issue with this step of building your foundation is that many people do not know what true friendship is. It is so sad to hear that many people are in friendships that are toxic and surface-level. They think that is all there is out there. The Bible talks a lot about friendship, thank goodness, which is why it is so important. Drew Hunter and Ray Ortlund wrote a book called *Made for Friendship*. The book "explores a biblical vision of true friendship . . . [and] demonstrates the universal need for friendship, what true friendship looks like, and how to cultivate deeper relationships." I highly recommend this to those who are trying to get better at viewing friendship as a positive thing. As the book says, the hard thing is that our culture is turning more and more into a lonely culture that values isolation over camaraderie.

My mom is naturally introverted, and when I brought up this topic of friendship, she said that even though she knows she needs friendship, it is hard to cultivate a time for it. She has three daughters, a needy dog, and two parents who are getting older and developing health concerns. I've talked to a lot of friends who are in their mid-30s, unmarried, and have little social interaction and experience. After the morning routines, a long day at work, and providing a healthy meal for you or your family, you are too exhausted to hold a Bible study or go out with friends because the next day you have to get up and do it all again. The monotony of each day is exhausting, and sometimes you cannot handle another thing on your plate. However, I believe the right type of friendship will make the monotony better and will revive you rather than exhaust you. I think the *who* and the *how* often get people feeling trapped and not wanting friendships.

After conversations with true friends, I feel ready to take on the day in light of the truth I was just fed. However, I have seen it done the opposite way where friends can become cumbersome if they do not truly understand what you are going through and ask more of you than you have to give. I think people have to determine whether or not certain activities wear them out or rejuvenate them. If you are cultivating friendships, maybe you need something to do rather than talking the entire time. Or maybe you just need to sit with a nice cup of coffee and read the Bible together. Time with others can also be part of your wind-down routine. It can be restful if you make it that way. It may also look different in different seasons, but we have to communicate that to our friends, say what would best serve us, and ask what would be best for them as well.

One of my professors once told me that she loves her friends, but they only meet twice a month and text occasionally. I think the transition of life stages warrants different amounts of time spent with friendships; however, what makes a good friendship does not change with circumstances. A good friend sticks by your side when you are going through a hard time. I think an example of bad friends is seen in Job where his friends, instead of caring for and walking with him in his struggles, belittled him for how he was struggling. In contrast, a true friend is kind and merciful, and graciously rebukes and guides our mistakes to the cross of Jesus, saying that there is life evermore.

A particular friend of mine is very honest and blunt. One day I made a careless remark that was untrue, and she called my bluff. I said about a picture posted for my birthday that it was "so sweet, and I cried my eyes out." It was a bit of an exaggeration, and my friend said honestly, "No, you did not. I was sitting right here." Although that was a simple and silly little thing, it made me think about the weight of my words and how I should say things I mean and not exaggerate. Later that night, my dear friend repented for talking about someone who was not there. It was nothing she would not have said herself, but my friend wanted to apologize about it since it did not add to the conversation. These moments showed me so much about how good friends repent and call out. These are not easy things to do, but they are needed and build friendship; they do not tear it apart.

Friends are a beautiful thing because they mean we have people in our court who root for us in all ways. The most important part of friendship is how it uplifts you and points you to Jesus. Jesus is our greatest friend, and He longs for us to use this life for Him. We can see him clearly in others and in the way He works with people around us. It is so encouraging to hear what He is doing in other people's lives. Why would we skip out on such a great opportunity to hear more about what Jesus is doing? It is life-giving because it is hope in conversation if you find it. Know that God wants you to find it, and thus He wants to give it to you. Be patient, and if you do not desire it right now, pray for the desire and the right people to be your friends.

The next part of preparing your foundation is making sure you "dig your foundation down to the frost line. Make sure the sides of your trench are vertical, square on the sides, and tamp down the bottom."[10] Each part of this is crucial, but I would argue that they are for our purposes, all talking about truth and aligning your beliefs with the Word of God. Hebrews 4:12 says, "For the word of God is living and active, sharper than any two-edged sword, piercing to the division

---

10 "Building a Stone Foundation," *This Cob House*, 2013, https://www.thiscobhouse.com/building-a-stone-foundation/.

of soul and of spirit, of joints and of marrow, and discerning the thoughts and intentions of the heart." However, we often do not treat it as living and active because it is not actively being lived out in our lives.

David Platt, a renowned pastor, gave a message at Passion 2023 where he quoted Psalm 138:2: "I bow down toward your holy temple and give thanks to your name for your steadfast love and your faithfulness, for you have exalted above all things your name and your word." He went on to recite Romans 1–8 from memory and said he used it as his sermon because we have to exalt God's name and His Word in our lives. We have to read His Word and worship just the words—without music, without lights, without anything—because they are worthy of praise; they are holy.

We have to treat God's Word as holy by exalting His name and His words in our lives. One of the ways we do that is by aligning our lives with God's Word. You may ask how to do that. It is quite simple. People shy away from doing this because it is a very daunting task to align every part of your life with every part of the Bible. However, all God asks us to do is read it, know it, and let Him do the rest. That is so freeing! We do not have to fix our lives to perfection. God wants our hearts and our willingness to let Him transform our hearts to His desires.

Building up the square sides of the foundation makes for a clear outline. I personally am not gifted with the side of art that uses paper and pencil, watercolor, or anything that has to be displayed accurately in picture form by free hand. My sisters and cousins got that gene that somehow skipped me and skipped me hard. So without the gift of visual art, my squares are not normally as clear and concise as they should be, and sometimes they even look like a circle. The reason they look like a circle is because the lines for circles can big or little and can even be sort of slanted and still look like a circle if you close the loop. When building in a circular shape, the pieces that were made for equal sides and clearly defined lines will not hold steady, and eventually the structure will not be stable. A square is equal on all sides, and thus the equation must check that the sides are multiplied by each other to make up the entirety of the square. I believe these can be the sides of the formula: church, community, worship, and quiet study. All these should influence the rest of our lives. However, the main point of the square is that it is vertical.

If your life is directed horizontally at something, it will not go where God wants it to go. He wants you to look up and let Him guide you. I think a good analogy is an airplane. To find the perfect square foundation, companies recommend using the Pythagorean theorem, which is most commonly used for triangles. A plane uses the horizontal to start, but the rest of the part of ascension is vertical. Why is that so? If they just went horizontally, even if they slightly lifted off the ground, they would run out of runway and crash into many things. God wants you to direct your gaze and all sides of your square (e.g., your life) toward Him, and then He causes you to move forward to create that angle—the C squared.

When you direct the base of your life upward, the structure will continue in that same manner. So build the sides up, and make sure they are clearly drawn with what the Bible says. We do not want any circles in our foundation.

Once you hold value for the truth and view it as such, be sure you know how hard you stand on it. I love coffee, and I got an espresso machine for Christmas. One of the things about making an espresso for a latte or just a simple espresso is the preparation of the grind. Once you put in the grind to your portafilter, you have to make sure the grind is evenly distributed (much like what we just talked about), and then you have to tamp the grinds down. To see how bad it would be, I once brewed the espresso and intentionally did not tamp the grinds down. All I got was water with a bit of coffee flavoring and a lot of the grind spilling out with the water. The good thing is that I could pour out the cup and put a new grind in. That, however, is not so easy to do with your life. Once you have dug out all your past hurts, misconceptions, and denials of the gospel and leveled yourself at the frontline to not let water distort your foundational lines, the last thing you want is to ruin all that just because you did not tamp down the truth.

A common saying is that pressure makes diamonds. I hate to say it, but it's true. Often when we learn who God is, who we are, and how He cares for us, it is not through mountaintops but in valleys. It is often in the hard places that He grows us the most. But let me give you a little hope. If you find yourself in a hard circumstance at the moment, know that He knows you. What does that mean? Well, in tamping for coffee and foundations, there is a point where too much tamping can be a bad thing. Putting too much pressure on the grinds or the ground can cause the surface to become uneven or even crack in the center. God knows your limit. He will never tamp something in so hard that you crack under the pressure. We are stubborn people if we are being honest with ourselves, so some things may take a bit more pressure to learn. But God knows how, when, why, and what you need in order to trust Him more. Whenever He tamps your life, you will know the truth, and you will be thankful for the pressure.

The final part of preparing your site is your drainage point. As we have already seen in this book, we do not want water seeping into the foundation since many types of cracks can form later on. So even though we think we are tamped enough not to let any water in (the schemes of the devil), the truth is that we are not, but God is. The devil is crafty. He is not going to scream in your face and tell you how he is going to tempt you away from God's grace. He is also always changing, so if he knows he cannot get you in a certain way, he will to try every trick up his sleeve in many different ways.

One way that water has only one way to get out of your foundation is to make a trench that slopes. The water has no permission to stay. In Louie Giglio's book *Don't Give the Enemy a Seat at Your Table*, he addresses the notion of filtering thoughts. Lies will enter, but we have to filter them down the sloped trench. Determining how you will drain the lies is key. There are a bunch of different tactics to use—talking to others, asking for prayer and accountability, having a prayer closet, writing out the lies on one side of a journal and the truths on the other side (counteracting the lies with scripture), praying, worshipping (I love a good nighttime car ride worship sesh), and taking every single thought captive by not letting them enter your mind.

Although this process of laying the foundation can be seen as tedious, painful, or just a long process, I guarantee you it is worth it. My friend told me an analogy she learned from her small group leader, and I will never forget it. Life is like a building block. God is at the bottom, and everything is built on Him. However, if you take out the bottom piece, the whole structure crumbles. Remaining strong in the Lord is not by our strength. Even aligning our life with His is not in our strength. Pray for the desire to be deepened, realigned, refined, and packed with truth. Let's use God's words as our sword and shield, and regard Him as the holiest thing in our lives.

Chapter 8
Gravel

Setting your foundation is crucial since it sets your heart as a foundation for God's plan and invites Him in so His work can be done through you without the weight crushing you. First, it comes by sorting out your stones or sorting out your life. This is seeing what fits inside your site preparation and what does not. It involves seeing which larger stones—parts of your life—contain the X—God—that marks them as worthy of holding up the key points of the structure.

Some parts of our lives contain God—the X—and others we think are too small to bother writing the X on them. But friend, let me tell you that each stone should have an X on it, no matter how small it is. A great analogy is that some people say that God fits within each little circle of our lives. However, it should be that God is the biggest circle, and the other circles that make up our lives fit into that big circle. That means we are not putting God into everything, but He makes up everything we do and is the base on which every circle operates.

Next are your batter boards. These are your methods of fighting and are tapered to fit your structure. God wants to reveal Himself to you, but to some that looks one way and to others it looks a completely different way. That is because God is constant but makes everything unique. I love getting up early and spending my quiet time then, but others operate better at night. There is no right way because God just wants to spend time with us. Maybe for some, praying is really hard with background music, and maybe the only way another person can pray is with some sort of background noise. Maybe you need to have your eyes completely shut to pray, or perhaps you need to have your eyes open and focused on something else, such as driving. The revealed nature of God is what all these batter boards are trying to do. It is a guideline laid out in Scripture that fits your structure as fighting points. God does not define ways to meet with Him as a one-size-fits-all. He loves you too much to do that. So do not try to fit a standard that is not placed by God for a specific way to commune with Him.

In a meeting with one of my mentors, I wanted to talk about a controversial topic in the church. She was informative and helpful with great insight into my church's stance on the topic. She works for the church and can explain the different levels of importance of topics to address and highlight as points of discussion in the church. The term is called *theological triage.* The third and not as important topics of controversy are subjects such as the style of worship or the structure of the church building. These topics are less important and do not affect the overall belief in the gospel. The second-order doctrines are the controversial topics that separate denominations and churches. An example would be women's role in the church. The first-order doctrines are known as the non-negotiables. "Without these doctrines, we either give up the gospel or put ourselves at risk of losing the gospel."[11] An example of this would be whether Jesus was just a man or the Messiah.

First-order doctrines are what make up the pillars of our faith. It might be hard to not base your belief on your specific denomination, but we have to get to the root and see that the first-level doctrines are the basis of what we need. We must get the simplest things down. We do not want a complicated foundation; we want one that is complete. "This Jesus is the stone that was rejected by you, the builders, which has become the cornerstone" (Acts 4:11). Don't be the builder who rejects the cornerstone. To make it complete in the Lord, we must level our corners on these four things:

1. God created everything and is still sovereign over everything He created (Gen. 1, Acts 17:24–25, 1 Tim. 6:15–16, Eph. 1:21–23, Matt. 28:18).

---

11 Samuel Emadi, "Theological Triage and the Doctrine of Creation," *The Gospel Coalition*, October 20, 2015, https://www.thegospelcoalition. org/article/theological-triage-and-the-doctrine-of-creation/.

2. Jesus is fully God and was fully man (1 Tim. 2:5,
    John 3:16, John 1:14, Col. 2:9, Acts 9:20, Luke
    1:31–33).

3. Jesus paid the price for all sins—past, present,
    and future (Rom. 6:23, John 12:30, Rom. 6:11,
    Gal. 3:26, Rom. 8:11, Rom. 5:6–11).

4. All will be made new in Christ when He returns
    to bring all things to completion to Himself for
    those who love, trust, and believe in Him (Phil.
    3:20–21, Phil. 1:6, 1 Cor. 1:8, 2 Tim. 2:11–13,
    John 17:3, Gal. 5:6, Eph. 1:5, Eph. 2:6, Phil. 3:20,
    Titus 2:11–14).

All these verses are what build the cornerstone of our
faith because it is built on the cornerstone of Christ. This
beautiful passage describes this perfectly:

As you come to him, a living stone rejected by men
but in the sight of God chosen and precious, you
yourselves like living stones are being built up as
a spiritual house, to be a holy priesthood, to offer
spiritual sacrifices acceptable to God through Jesus
Christ. For it stands in scripture: 'Behold, I am laying
in Zion in a stone, a cornerstone chosen and precious,
and whoever believes in him will not be put shame.'
So the honor is for you who believe, but for those who
do not believe, 'The stone that the builders rejected

has become the cornerstone,' and 'A stone of stum-
bling, and a rock of offense.' They stumble because
they disobey the word, as they were destined to do.
                                                    —1 Pet. 2:4–8

God is our cornerstone that levels us, and all the stones
above are the defining characteristics of faith in the gospel
that leads us to trust in the cornerstone more.

The Face You Want

The next fact about foundation-laying made my jaw drop at
how directly it correlates. "Lay your stones so that the 'face'
that you want is showing on the outside of your foundation
wall. Try to use faces that have a slight upward slope to them.
This will help shape your wall nicely."[12] We all project an
image, and I'm not talking about a physical image. Have you
ever noticed that a person can be drop-dead gorgeous on the
outside, but their personality makes what would be a 10 a
solid 4? Our bodies are merely a temporary home for our
souls to dwell in. Our souls have the ability to project the
image of many things, but the only truly beautiful thing is
God.

Jealousy, comparison, greed, pride, slander, and all
other sinful attributes do not show the image of God. So it

12 "Building a Stone Foundation," *This Cob House*, 2013, https://www.
thiscobhouse.com/building-a-stone-foundation/.

is important to ask yourself whose image you are displaying. Does your image make others want to look to Christ? I can confidently say that my answer to that question on a daily basis is no. We will never be Christ, but we can possess the fruit of the Spirit by spending time with Him and letting His power shine through us, despite our shortcomings. That's the gracious God we serve, that even if we do not reflect His image every day, He wants to refine and sanctify us to look more like Him every moment and through every learning experience. Although trials are not so fun, He is purging our face to look more like His, and that takes some letting go of sinful attributes and carving our stone to have an upward slope.

Our upward slope means that even though we do not always look like Jesus and do not always live in a way that is pleasing to the Lord, He invites us to look up. Those two words—look up—hold a lot of power. Looking up causes us to stop looking in and self-analyzing. Looking up causes us to see the problem-solver and focus on His heavenly attributes. But here is the real and convicting thing. We cannot look like God if we do not know Him. That's why having that upward slope will shape you to know that even though you will fail, you look up, and He is right there to show you Himself.

Contact

Have you ever played the game Red Rover? Well, if you have not, here is a quick summary of it. Two groups of people line up on two sides. Both groups link up as tightly and as strongly as they can. One side then agrees to send one of their members to the other side to run and try to break the bond of the group that called them by saying, "Red Rover, Red Rover, send _____ over." As this person charges with full force, the team tries to stand their ground as strongly as possible and as tightly as they can, all linked together. However, if you played the game in elementary or middle school, the inevitable happened; a girl got stuck next to a boy she thought had cooties, and they would not touch at that moment unless the world ended. Thus, the person running at them chose them to run through because that was the path of least resistance.

This is very similar to foundations and more importantly to the Christian faith. All the stones have to have contact. The Bible is concrete, and there are no holes, so everything is connected there. That's a great thing. Furthermore, the problem is not with the Bible or God's commitment to us; it is with us. I would imagine that there are some parts of the Bible or God's character that do not make sense to you. But you cannot let what does not make sense keep you from accepting it as truth. The devil will attempt to make you question what God says and what you know is true, to the point that you think that a stone has cooties and therefore you are hesitant to fully make contact with it. So the devil chooses to bulldoze through and break your connection completely. Perhaps it is just in general that we have not chosen to connect, or maybe we have not strongly connected to Him and His truth. So when the devil comes in at full speed because he won't slow down for you, we lose connection. Don't lose contact with God; He wants to link your arms with His truth and fight for you, but you cannot do that if you do not contact Him and touch His truth.

Hearting

You may be asking the same question as I did when I first read about hearting. What is hearting? Well, I was shocked at this metaphor. It is like God orchestrated every single thing back to Himself to show how we are supposed to build our lives on Him. I think it is so amazing that our God shows us Himself in everything He makes. It is all for us to glorify Him and for our good. Hearting is "smaller stones or gravel to help support the large stones and fill in the gaps."[13] Let's be clear. There are no gaps in the truth of God, but when laying the foundation for your life, there is a possibility for gaps. Hang with me, and I will explain.

The Bible says that the Spirit will fill the gaps where understanding is not humanly possible. "And the Spirit of the Lord shall rest upon him, the Spirit of wisdom and understanding, the Spirit of counsel and might, the Spirit of knowledge and the fear of the Lord" (Isa. 11:2). This is talking about how the Spirit rests on Jesus, spoken as the stump

---

13 "Building a Stone Foundation," *This Cob House*, 2013, https://www.thiscobhouse.com/building-a-stone-foundation/.

of Jesse; however, that same spirit lives in us (Rom. 8:11). The Spirit can use different things to fill in the gap. God loves each of His children steadfastly and made them each unique. The best part of that is that He knows you fully. So He knows that stirring up a deeper love for Himself means meeting with someone for coffee, deep prayer, or long and extensive worship. All these things are beautiful and good for building a stable foundation.

As beautiful as these heartings are, they can pose an issue. Two problems arise when the hearting is forced in or when there are more heartings than the larger stones. When the hearting is forced in, it can disturb the positions of the larger stones, and when there are more heartings than large stones, shifting will occur. If worship, prayer, and godly conversation are forced, there is a potential to focus too much on those things and desire to participate in them even if they aren't in any way fitting. You end up resenting the larger stones and thus disturb their positioning. In contrast, there is the temptation to rely on the little stones too much and stop laying larger stones all together, relying solely on encounters and not on the alive and active Word of the Lord. There has to be an appropriate balance of truth and Spirit-filled encounters, conversations, prayers, and worship.

Static

The last thing we will address is static stone laying. This is a type of systematic laying that allows you to lay stone onto a string line that is attached to the batter boards in order to keep you going up at the right slope. The line is godly wisdom. I recommend getting a godly mentor in your life. Life is hard, and having someone with perhaps a lot more life experience than you will help show you the way through personal experiences and trials. I have been blessed with many mentors in my life, all with many more years more than I. Psalm 145:4 says, "One generation shall commend your works to another, and shall declare your mighty acts." To be mentored is a beautiful thing because both people can spur hope in each other, telling each other of God's great deeds.

The Importance of Gravel

"The skill of the worker is what holds your stonework together."[14] Know that you have the most perfect worker—Jesus. He knows you, loves you, and longs to hold you together through Himself. He wants not only to start your build but to cover you. My encouragement to you is to let not only His truth but His love cover you as well. He wants you to lean into His loving peace that grants perfect rest.

The most important part of laying the stones is knowing the gravel and the nature of your gravel. The basics recommend that you "lay down a few inches of gravel on the

---

14 "Building a Stone Foundation," *This Cob House*, 2013, https://www. thiscobhouse.com/building-a-stone-foundation/.

bottom of your trench and tamp it down, use drain-grade gravel."[15] Let me assure you that God is a drain-grade gravel. The definition of *tamping* according to Merriam Webster is to drive in or down by a succession of light or medium blows. This is uncomfortable but necessary. God often shows Himself in beautiful ways, but seeing His ways, trusting in Him, and truly learning who He is often takes a bit more convincing. We are such stubborn and fickle people; we often learn things the hard way.

The best thing, though, is that we are not only laying all our stones on top of the character of God, but we are also being covered by more gravel, more of Him. He not only wants to build us on Him but cover us with Himself. He drains so much from us and protects us from cracking, often in ways we do not even know or see. He also covers our foundation that He wants to preserve with Himself, so we know that none of our preservation is in our hands. Gravel is filling every layer before the big stones to protect the truth that He wants to build you upon.

Mortaring

Mortar is essentially the glue, but there are certain aspects of the glue that make things stick or not—a correlation to faith. I recently got a giving key as a birthday gift when I took a trip

---

15 "Building a Stone Foundation," *This Cob House*, 2013, https://www. thiscobhouse.com/building-a-stone-foundation/.

to visit my friend in Nashville. If you have never had a giving key, I encourage you to get one, but just be prepared to be challenged. The giving key reads, "Embrace your word, then pay it forward to a person you feel needs the message more than you." The "key" to the giving key is "giving" it away. However, I argue that one of the biggest parts is learning how the key works so you can teach someone else. I got a key of hope recently at a cute philanthropy shop in Nashville. I was really excited to give it to my friend, but I felt convicted by a sermon to keep it and learn it first before I threw off the responsibility of learning it and the potentially painful process it could bring about. I did not want this, but God knew I needed it. I started to see that even though I was hopeful for others in conversation, I had no hope for myself. I would often talk about how others have great things coming for them from God, but I didn't believe that could or would ever happen to me.

My comments seemed small to me, but God wanted to fix that root. He wanted me to learn what hope looks like and what it means to live that out. I was watching a sermon, and the pastor encouraged everyone, instead of automatically sharing the message, to sit with it, let it take root, and see what it is like to apply it. When applying the mortar, you must let it sit and settle before you put any weight on it. Mortar can take anywhere from 28 hours to four weeks to set. This reminds me of God's perfect timing. I can expect to learn how to be hopeful in a week and then give it to my friend, but God may have and probably does have a completely different plan. For those God has been preparing for a while to learn a certain attribute of Himself, it might only take them 28 hours. But if it takes you four weeks or even four years, know that it's how long God wanted it to take. When you truly learn about it and it sets in, you realize it is a consistent learning process and a daily surrender in order to keep hope alive as you trust in God and surrender all to Him.

We are always going to be students of the Word, but we have hope because we have the best and most loyal Teacher. This Teacher knows that this road we are walking is in the world, so it is hard. But He won't apply any weight until you are fully set on the things He knows you need—the next stone to rest sturdily on you. You can also have hope because you know the weight never fully rests on you. God knows we are fallen and not meant to hold the world's weight. My wise cousin once said to me as I was expressing my hopelessness in the world, "You know, we were not meant to fix the world, just witness to it." God does not expect us to fix the whole world; He just calls us to be faithful to what is in our hands. This is hard to do when we see that the things in our hands are taking too long to settle in and become set in our hearts. That is where trust in God's strength and perfect timing takes effect.

Timing and Abiding

Something I am baffled by is the sheer majesty of our God. Time is not lost to Him, yet it does not apply to Him. He knows the perfect moments to teach us and introduce different things in different areas and at different times of our life. He is not bound by time but cares about us being inside the bounds of time. He also knows that it takes time to abide. First John 2:24 says, "Let what you heard from the beginning abide in you. If what you heard from the beginning abides in you, then you too will abide in the Son and in the Father." What is good about abiding? It is good because it means that as we learn more about what God has been teaching us, we learn who He is, which is the end goal. He then gives us the greatest gift from that abiding—getting to abide with Him forever. First John 2:25 says, "And this is the promise that he made to us—eternal life." That is the best promise that God is eager to fulfill. All He teaches us is about getting an eternal perspective, so do not despise what He is growing you in. It will be worth it.

A noteworthy thing is a power God has already given you. If you are in Christ, you have been given the Spirit, the same one that raised Jesus Christ from the dead. The Spirit gives us a spirit of discernment if we lean in and listen. It later says in 1 John 2:27. "But the anointing that you received from him abides in you, and you have no need that anyone should teach you. But as his anointing teaches you about everything, and is true, and is no lie—just as it has taught you, abide in him." You have a royal inheritance, and God wants to invite you to see a glimpse of that inheritance. By abiding in Him, we will have the eyes to see it more clearly. So lean in, and have hope.

I'm sure I have mentioned this before, but the word I feel called to focus on for this year is *holy*—holy in sense of seeing God as holy and how viewing Him as such affects every aspect of our lives. At a worship event with my church's staff, we brought in Aaron Williams, writer of the song "Abide," to lead worship for us and share a bit of what the Lord delights to do with His children, which is simply to be with them. During the worship night, I felt called to go up afterward and ask what Aaron had learned about God's holiness. Aaron is amazing, and I now consider him a brother in Christ and a friend, even though I only had one conversation with him. (I encourage you to be like this to anyone who comes up; just be a friend because you never know how it can change someone's life.) Aaron told me that before he truly started abiding with God, he would come off stage after leading worship and want the audience's approval. He said until he started recognizing that every moment of praising the Lord was an invitation to His holiness and to see Him for the good God that He is, he always sought others' approval. But once he started viewing it as intentional time with his Father, he saw holiness and less of himself. He was abiding rather than seeking approval. This is true of all life. We then talked about the goodness of God to invite His children to abide and hear God's heart in order to not feel the need to search anymore for anything else but find fulfillment in the holiness of our Father.

As you see and learn more of God's heart—so much that all your life consumes and pours out His goodness—you become less focused on all the things that need fixing and start to focus on the Fixer and Sustainer who has the end secured. John tells us that in his first letter. I love John's confidence in God when he talks about learning the new covenant and seeing the light of God. "At the same time, it is a new commandment that I am writing to you, which is true in him and in you, because the darkness is passing away and the true light is already shining" (1 John 2:8). The truth is shining, and the devil is trying to put a basket on that light. But we have to fixate on that light, lift the basket, have hope, and see that the dark can never be dark enough to block out the light that God wants to shine on us and in us. But know that to have the hope and confidence like John had, we have to know the light and abide in the light to see through the magnifying glass of God's Word, His holiness, and an overall good plan.

Chapter 9
Clay Foundation

Here is why this book is called *Rock or Clay*. I'm sure you have heard that Northern states have soil that is built on rock, and in the South, there is a foundational clay soil. That is why people in the South cannot have basements. If you have been in church a while, you know the classic story about the house built on the rock and the house built on the sand. We'll talk about this story in a bit, but first I want to show you the actual construction of building houses on rock or on clay.

I argue that both rock and clay soils are beneficial, but I believe there are times when we must move to rocky soil. Most clay minerals are extracted from some sort of weathering or erosion. They can vary in size and usually stem from preexisting minerals. I believe this is for the believer who is just now coming to the faith. There are things the Lord uses. Sometimes it's people constantly inviting someone to church, or maybe it's a loss in the family that caused you to look to God. But all in all, we know that God wants you to see there is a time and a place for everything.

> For though by this time you ought to be teachers, you need someone to teach you again the basic principles of the oracles of God. You need milk, not solid food, for everyone who lives on milk is unskilled in the word of righteousness, since he is a child. But solid food is for the mature, for those who have their powers of discernment trained by constant practice to distinguish good from evil.
>
> —Heb. 5:12–14

Pure milk is and should be the desire of your soul upon first hearing of God's grace and resting in His freedom. First Peter 2:2–3 says, "Like newborn infants, long for the pure spiritual milk, that by it you may grow up into salvation— if indeed you have tasted that the Lord is good." It is good that we have tasted and seen. There is a time to be filled, but there is also a time to pour out.

Another characteristic of clay is that it soaks up a lot of water and expands upon contact with water. This is a great thing, but it has the potential to become too full and take the shape of the structure it rests on, causing erosion and the differential settlement we talked about earlier. The house cannot always rest on this soil because "the process by which some clay minerals swell when they take up water is reversible. Swelling clay expands or contracts in response to changes in environmental factors, [and it] can be developed safely with minimal effects on the environment."[16] I know these facts both sound great, but I will explain why they are not ideal.

First, this is the potential for Christians who are content staying surface level with God or are in the beginning stages of their faith. There is a temptation to stay in this space, partly because it does not require a lot of upkeep. Clay minerals are often found at the top or near the surface of the earth, meaning it is easy. Christianity has never been known to be easy. This does not mean there are no good moments; it just means it is not an easy or popular decision, especially in our day and age. The clay swells and shrinks with changing weather and causes cracks if the change is very small. We have seen how those tiny cracks can actually cause a lot of problems. But these are the things the devil wants for us. He wants us to change and be the fickle people we are by changing our approach to everything with each change of season or environment. This constant change means we are not resting on the unchanging nature of God. Let's be real. We are not constant, and each changing season can sometimes require a new outlook. But our foundation should not swell or shrivel based on the atmospheric effect of the season.

---

16 Nora Kay Foley, "Environmental Characteristics of Clays and Clay Mineral Deposits," *U.S. Geological Survey*, 1999, https://doi.org/10.3133/70220359.

In every season, we rest on God and see that we should not shrivel back due to the dryness of the atmosphere around us. I am guilty of this at times too. I just got convicted as I wrote that sentence because I want to run away instead of speak life when it feels dry around me because it is hard. This wishy-washy, circumstantial faith, however, is a faith the devil is not scared of. Do you want the devil to fear you? You need to walk out in the freedom God has granted you and live like God has won, because He has. This surface-level Christianity takes the form of the other clay around it and does not seek to go deeper, and thus the environment is not greatly affected by it. God called us to be the salt and light of the earth. Thus we cannot stay in the comfortable; He wants us to lean fully on Him.

Another scary attribute of clay is that "a mixture of a lot of clay and a little water results in mud that can be shaped and dried to form a relatively rigid solid. This property is exploited by potters and the ceramics industry to produce plates, cups, bowls, pipes, and so on. Environmental industries use both these properties to produce homogeneous liners for containment of waste."[17] With a little water, all can be shaped. I love the use of the word *exploited*. That is exactly what the devil will do. He wants to steal, kill, and destroy you. I hate to be so blunt, but you have to know how badly

---

17 Nora Kay Foley, "Environmental Characteristics of Clays and Clay Mineral Deposits," *U.S. Geological Survey*, 1999, https://doi. org/10.3133/70220359.

he wants you to have no hope and no life, and to stop moving toward the Kingdom. He wants to take you out, so he is
going to exploit everything to make you a rigid solid that is
hardened to the goodness of God and thus can only contain
the things of the world that are waste. If he can get you to
resent the things God has put in your hands so much that
you let it all go, he will quickly come and fill your life with
waste, which won't look like waste at first. Don't accept what
he wants to give you. Search deeper. God wants you to be
firm on Him, making you solid and stable, not rigid.

So now that we have established that clay is not something you want as your foundation, we can now talk about
the soil composition we want to build our lives on. It is
actually what I have explained this whole time—the soil we
should build on. We mustn't miss this. As I have mentioned
before, this soil requires more upkeep and careful conduct,
but know that it can be repaired if you simply trust in the
One who made the blueprints. Know that waterproofing
is not beneficial for the foundation, and repointing and
proper drainage are necessary. It's much like moving to
the North where we turn our gaze up to the higher beau-
ties that God invites us to move up to by becoming deeply
rooted in Him.

Basements show the deep structure that is rooted in
Jesus. They have the crucial pumps to drain out the schemes
of the devil and the mortar refill to relearn the things God
has taught us in the past. These basements are only possible
because of the rocky soil on which the house is built. The

rock soil may require a few repairs since time and weathering can cause some mortar to flake off, but it is more stable than clay in the long run, thus keeping your house aligned and sturdy. "The material under the foundation (usually soil) is the actual load-bearing system that supports the house. Some types of soil, such as sand and gravel, can be good for supporting a house. Loose fill can't support heavy loads, for example. And clay-rich soil can expand and contract with changes in moisture levels, causing a foundation to settle or walls to crack from inward pressure."[18] This is the system that will hold all the weight, so we have to be very careful when setting the first most crucial weight so it can hold up the rest. I know this can seem tedious, but I assure you, the sooner we address this issue in our lives and work to build sustainable, weight-bearing soil, we will be set since we will be standing on God's made and prepared soil. The best news is that all soil is from God and thus orchestrated by Him to hold you up to whatever comes your way. But when we try to put our own mixture into the soil or even try to place a weight that was not intended for the soil, our whole house could crumble.

Believe me, this is a lot easier said than done. I am actively trying to work on this myself. It is also helpful to know that no one can ever truly learn everything. The lead

18 "House Foundations: Types and Common Problems," *This Old House*, n.d., https://www.thisoldhouse.com/foundations/21071846/house-foundations.

teaching pastor of a church called Redeemer, a small church in Lubbock, Texas, gave an analogy one Sunday morning of everyone trying to push a boulder up a hill each day, only for it to roll down on top of them at night. How often do we do this? We try so hard to push the boulder up all on our own each day, only for it to fall right back down. Why does this happen? It is because we were never made or meant to do the pushing alone. When God is pushing and holding it up, He stops at a good place. He is our guide rather than our backup plan. A picture the Lord allowed me to think of when the pastor was painting this analogy was God pushing up the boulder and me holding on tightly to Jesus with my head buried into Him, afraid to look, and my feet barely moving. This picture humbled and granted peace all at the same time. It is hard to think that we cannot do anything, but it is also so freeing to know that when we let God lead, He has promised He will lead us to life.

Often when we rely on other soils than God, the process takes longer to build on than expected. It also costs a lot more because we don't think about what we are building on. We don't even think that this step is a stone or sand for something else to rest on. The question now is whether it will sink or stand. Sometimes the reason we don't consider the other implications is that we don't have a track record to refer to. God has the most perfect track record. It has a perfect gift of faithfulness wrapped in a beautiful ribbon of His grace. I don't know about you, but I would rather build my life on that beauty and watch what beauty God decides to build than risk it on something that could end in destruction and not promote construction.

House on the Rock, Not the Sand

Everyone then who hears these words of mine and does them will be like a wise man who built his house on the rock. And the rain fell, and the floods came, and the winds blew and beat on that house, but it did not fall, because it had been founded on the rock. And everyone who hears these words of mine and does not do them will be like a foolish man who built his house on the sand. And the rain fell, and the floods came, and the winds blew and beat against that house, and it fell, and great was the fall of it.

—Matt. 7:24–27

This love in which God first loved us loves us enough to not let us be washed away by the waves He wants to prepare us for. Everything before this section in Matthew 7 contains an underlying but also very prominent theme of eternity. Books such as *Pilgrims Progress* and *Driven by Eternity* put into perspective Matthew 7:13–14 that says, "Enter by the narrow gate. For the gate is wide and the way is easy that leads to destruction, and those who enter by it are many. For the gate is narrow and the way is hard that leads to life, and those who find it are few." God assures us that it will be hard, and we are not promised ease, but He promises

Himself, which is a billion times better than any ease we can fathom.

As I am writing this section of the book, I am visiting my sister in Lubbock, Texas. If you have ever been to Lubbock or heard about Lubbock, you know that the wind is beyond comprehension. As I sit by my sister's fireplace, I hear the roaring sound of the wind through the fireplace and then shoving its way against the wall. I also see the clouds of dust roll over the location where my sister's apartment is. I had heard of this but never witnessed it for myself, and let me tell you, it is something else. As I think about it more, though, I heard it but didn't witness it, and that is where it can get tricky. People hear about the pounding wind, and when they experience it, their foundation is not sturdy, and they want to run.

However, on the flip side, if you do build your house on the Lord and on His promise, even though rain, wind, and raging storms will come, you know you are secure. But notice that I heard the wind and saw the dark cloud over the area. As I sit at the airport watching the sky turn intense shades of orange from the swept-up dust, I contemplate how even the sight or hearing of it can make you feel like you are going to topple over. Sometimes the storm around you rages and the clouds are so thick that you cannot see past the next day, but you know that God has you. You built your house on Him, so you are safe within His arms. Even as the glass is shaking and looks as though it will break, you know He is unchanged and unfazed, and knew all along that this would happen.

I never thought this would happen, but I am so joyous, believe it or not. My flight got canceled, and I might have to spend the night at the airport if the wind does not calm down. I feel the biggest peace about it. It is a troubling situation for so many, and I am able to encourage and speak with them, which is a situation I prayed for—to be able to speak to people at the airport. I know that is a weird prayer, but you have no idea who needs this. I am thankful to say all of this because my house is built on the Lord, which is none of my doing. It has been all through His continually snapping me back to fix my eyes on Him because I cannot do anything else.

We must steady our minds on things that are above and see that God is above everything we are facing. We must study His Word and practice what it says. You may ask, how can we practice peace? Joy? Love? Goodness? And all the other fruits that do not seem to have an action attached to the practicing of the good thing. But God promises that He is the best thing, and if we abide in Him, He will bring completion to all those things in us. We practice peace, joy, goodness, and love by living in it. We live in it because we know it. We live from a knowledge of holding the truth that brings life to death. We hold the truth, live it, and dwell in it because we know that to live apart from it is to give way to the harsh winds of the world and not make an impact by being the only thing that seems steady.

God is mighty. He has the strength to not only hold you but withstand you during the trials you are going through.

I would rather trust in a sure hope than one that is blowing with the wind. Anyone who builds their house on the immovable foundation of God and His truth is set and sure because their hope is not set in the world or even how things turn out. Their hope is set on the One who has won and the One who has the future secure, looking to a day when there will be no more tears, no more heartache, no more sickness, and no more hurt. All will be made right even if it isn't right now. Resting in that hope takes trusting so much in His word that nothing, not even the worst thing in the world, can strip you of your inheritance.

This is not easy to see at the moment, and that's why the Lord will prepare you with many things to show that even in the hard times, He is still God, and He is still holding you. God created you and is building you up in Himself, and He knew that things would happen. So when He allows you to walk through trying things, know that He is preparing you for something or that this is your something and that He is calling you to step into it. It is the next day, and I felt as though the Lord was calling me to finish this book this weekend, which I thought was crazy. The Lord makes things happen in His timing and in His way, even when we think it cannot be done. As I sit here, though, I look up at the sign that is above my head that says "Learning is a team sport." As cheesy as that is, it is true.

As I texted one of my dear friends to ask about what to pray for her, she asked me that same question but also took it a step further. She asked me how I was working to apply the things I was learning. Although I was working on figuring it all out, I hadn't put it into words so someone could be praying, not just for the thing to be learned but for the practical application of it. Accountability is so good; it takes trust, but in the end, it will leave you feeling known, and it will keep you learning. Learning is how we build.

The most freeing and sometimes frustrating thing is the truth that we are not perfect. God created us to constantly be learning—learning more about Him, His Word, and His people. This is hard to do when we do not see God as the rock and when we are not sure of who He is. When we feel betrayed by God letting things happen to us, by His Word saying things that are controversial to popular belief, and by His people, we can grow cynical and not trust the rock. But we must know that He is not the issue—our fallenness is. Countless times in the Bible, the priest, Moses, and others who encountered God had to cover their eyes from His majesty.

If we cannot accurately see God in His form right now, it is not far off that we cannot accurately see His glory in all things. But we must pray for God's insight, His eyes, and His way to be carved out as a clear path. Even if it is narrow, we know it is sturdy. God will not fade like the sand. He built the mountains to incredibly high heights that are incomprehensible to mankind, but He did it. He did it to show that a sturdy, widespread, and level base can be built up to leave people in awe. That's what He longs to do with us.

God wants people to look at us and see something

different. He wants people to look at us and see that we are not easily distraught by circumstances but are firm in Him. He wants us to do everything He places in our hands—big or small—with so much of His love, joy, and peace that people cannot help but wonder and be drawn to it. So be faithful to what is right in front of you, and do not let it slip through your hands like sand because that is not what you are built on. If you wake up, there is an opportunity. We just have to be alive and awake to it. Please, Lord, wake us up to stand firm on You.

It's hard to see at times, but the kindness of God is so evident that we don't even have to sift through the fineness of the sand; we know the soundness of the rock. We see God's goodness and unchangeable nature even though we change constantly. So why do we not trust that God will be faithful still? I believe there is not one correct answer to that question. For every person, every story, and every move, we have the ability to continue out of a place of uncertainty because of a multitude of different things. But I encourage you to talk to the person you trust most in your life and share why you feel held back from casting all your cares on the One who cares for you (1 Pet. 5:7). He does not want you to feel like all hope is lost, and it won't be if you place all hope on Him.

Fine sand has the ability to be so fine that it cracks quickly and cannot hold any weight. God wants to take the weight, and He is not fragile. Jesus defeated death just so He could write your name in His book of life and eventually call you home to Him. One question I have had is this: Why isn't He calling us all home yet? I then think of the countless number of people who have yet to hear of the greatest Comforter, the greatest Healer, the greatest Friend, and the greatest Hope we can find rest in. This gift we have knowledge of has yet to be given to some, and not receiving the most important gift will reap the worst consequence. We are standing strong on God, so what can harm us? That's right—absolutely nothing. What do we have to lose by sharing Him? Sharing Him could be the greatest gain for some, and we have everything in Him. Even if they do not accept it, you have planted a seed that the Lord wants to water.

We tend to take on a lot as a people. This can cause us to feel like we have to do everything to share the gospel. God simply wants to talk to people through us. One word you could say to someone could make the difference God wants to use in order for their eyes to be open to something outside themselves. So stand strong on Him, and trust that He is building you up to heighten His name and strike awe in others for who He is—a God of miracles and a personable God who loves more deeply than anything displayed in the here and now.

Chapter 10

Here I Am, Send Me

By wisdom a house is built,
and by understanding it is established.

—Prov. 24:3

W hat, why, and how are you wanting to build? Your house is not lost on God. He wants to provide you with all wisdom and insight into His Word so He can build you up on wisdom. Understanding is the way He wants to bring all the knowledge you have to fruition. Do you ever feel like you have not been established—in your town? on your job? with your finances? even at your church? There is a way to stay stagnant in your wisdom. It is by not taking time to understand it and apply it. You may have built your house's foundation, but if you have ever built your house, you know that once the foundation is set and the frame is put in place, the process seems to speed along.

This is not saying that if you apply your knowledge you will know everything about God, have ease, and convert many people. But it will be easier to apply it once you have the foundation set. If there is only the foundation and no one decides or knows how to build on it, it serves as a glimpse of what it is supposed to accomplish. We have to take the knowledge and gain understanding and insight from prayer, fasting, community, mentors, family, and time spent with our Savior. God wants to use us as His vessel, but we have to apply the things He whispers to us in His Word and many other ways so He can give us a greater understanding of what living for Him looks like. He wants to establish you in Himself, but we have to be open to learning and truly learn what active wisdom looks like.

Woe to him who builds his house by unrighteousness,
and his upper rooms by injustice,
who makes his neighbor serve him for nothing
and does not give him his wages,
who says, "I will build myself a great house
with spacious upper rooms,"
who cuts out windows for it,
paneling it with cedar
and painting it with vermilion.

—Jer. 22:13–14

God wants you to build your life on Him. He wants to build your life on His words and His way. A day in His courts, a day in His house, a single moment with Him in the upper room in His presence is life-giving, so He invites you in. What is concerning is how little we pay attention to His righteousness and His justice and go by what the world or our peers tell us. Building on His set guidelines is what is best and what will provide rest. God does not want you to build a mansion; He wants you to build a mission house that allows room for a lot of people to hear of His wonderful works. So do not build from a place of complacency; build from His righteousness and out of times of meeting with Him. He wants to show you Himself. Commune with Him, rest in Him, and trust in His judgments that produce righteousness.

You looked for much, and behold, it came to little. And when you brought it home, I blew it away. Why? declares the Lord of hosts. Because of my house that lies in ruins, while each of you busies himself with his own house.

—Hag. 1:9

We are a people who are always seeking. We seek pleasure and comfort. We seek lesser things that are worth little, but God wants us to long for more. He calls us to seek Him above all else. The goodness of the Lord is sure; it is set. It is set on heavenly things, not on the things of this world. We know little of what is good, but God holds all goodness. This verse holds true, especially in our day and age. Our society is constantly chasing after so much and so many things that ultimately will not amount to anything. When the Lord sees that we are holding onto so many things that are of lesser value than He is, He wants to show us that He is better and will give us much even if we have little.

God sees the things we so often chase after and seeks to free us of that. He blows what is meaningless out of our hands because He knows that what He holds and wants to give us is better. One of my favorite drawings is a beautiful image that depicts the abundance of trust we can have in Jesus but sadly do not. It shows a little girl holding a small teddy bear and saying, "But I love it, God." Jesus, the other figure in the image, is holding a giant teddy bear behind His back. He says, "Just trust me." Then He reaches out for the girl to hand him her small teddy bear so He can give her the bigger one behind His back.

This is exactly how we are. We think we know and want to hold on to things we think are good for us. But God has a greater insight, longs to show you Himself, and wants to give you something so much better. The scary part is that we cannot see that it is better when we give it to Him. We just have to trust Him. Trusting in Him is hard, not easy, but it is worth it. He wants us to see Him as more than enough and be satisfied with the things in His house.

We need to put God as the builder of our house but also recognize that His house is higher than ours and worthy of our utmost attention. God's house is made up of all our houses. The church is not a building; it's a people. We need to make our lives a building for Him that invites others in and builds up the body. Don't worry about building up your life on earth. Worry about being a fortress built by God where people can find peace, rest, and welcoming arms. That is what the Bible tells us is the greatest commandment—to love God and love others.

> For Jesus has been counted worthy of more glory than Moses—as much more glory as the builder of a house has more honor than the house itself.
> —Heb. 3:3

The house God builds for the Lord and on the Lord is more beneficial than the house. The home does not get the recognition. The One who built the home and wrote the blueprints for the home gets the recognition. This is as if your home couldn't have been designed without an idea. The Lord ordained an idea for you to be His, and He knit you together in your mother's womb. He wants you to know that He holds you tightly and loves you endlessly. He wants you to want people to praise Him through you. We just must recognize that He deserves all the glory for everything.

> Unless the Lord builds the house,
> Those who build it labor in vain.
> Unless the Lord watches over the city,
> The watchman stays awake in vain.
> —Ps. 127:1

The Lord must build your house. I cannot emphasize that enough. We cannot build it on our own effort. If we try to build the house, we labor in vain. If God builds it, it is sustained. The Lord must also guide it. After our house is built, we must look to take care of what God has placed in us.

God is looking to prepare something that people will wonder at. But after it is prepared, it must be kept as precious. Be careful to not let the devil quench your light. God wants to show it because He built it, prepared it, and sustains it. As I sit here and wait another seven hours for a plane to take me back to Dallas, I see an elderly woman standing and looking out at a plane that is about to depart. Her child is on that plane, and a single tear trickles down her cheek. She shakes her head as she sadly sits next to her husband. I imagine that this is how God feels about us. He made us, built us, prepared us, and sends us off to bring others to Himself, except He is on the plane with us. But that kind of love that watches their child leave on an airplane and then cries is the love God has for us. So imagine when one of His children sees the crack in their foundation, lets it slip, does not care to repair it, and turns to the world.

One of my dear friends once wrote me 19 things to remember for my 19th birthday. One of those things was that God's heart breaks when mine does. He longs to be with us when it is hard. He wants to build and sustain us, so we do not have to do it on our own. From my experience of trying to do it all alone, I know we need to let God in. He is your biggest cheerleader, and he loves you dearly. He wants to lift you up to see His perspective. It's much like a father lifting his child above his shoulders and letting them sit on top to see what he sees. You can see the child's excitement and wonder at the new perspective they have gained. That is exactly what the Lord wants to do. He wants you to trust Him with a child-like faith that reaches up so He can lift you up to see what He sees. In order to get His view and a glimpse of Him, we have to reach, trust, and regard our faith as something to be treasured, because it is. "For every house is built by someone, but the builder of all things is God" (Heb. 3:4). I love this verse because it ties this all together. You can build your house, but God built you and wants to build it on Himself. Do not neglect the Maker of everything. He builds, restores, and tears down. I want Him to build my life on His, restore my trust in Him, and tear down the ways I have operated out of pride, self-righteousness, selfishness, thinking I can do it all, fear, and a longing for comfort. God wants to build you. My advice is to let Him.

God built up His people in Egypt and delivered them. He helped Noah build an ark that was bigger than anyone had ever seen. He sent his only Son to be born as a baby. God who knew no form took on the form of humanity to take the sins of all humanity. The sins of humanity were then placed on Him and forgiven. Jesus then defeated death and the grave and gave hope to all the world. This is God just simply wanting you to spend time with Him.

The crucial questions we ask are what, why, and how. These are very good questions, but God wants us to trust Him and simply say, "Yes, God, I'm yours. He promises Himself to us sacrificially every day for always. God simply wants us to say the same thing. But He knows we are not perfect and will thus not want to say yes every day. But we must have tasted and seen His goodness.

Once we see and know that God is good, we can see and know that He holds us. He wants you to excavate all the things you tried to hold together and build yourself, and hand them to Him. Allowing God to renew that soil and show you how to actually build on Him will allow you to see that He is the Master Builder. He loves you and longs to make you strong in Him. It may take a bit to know how to release it all to Him, but He will help you at every stage of the process, even when letting it all go.

The point of building a firm foundation is all about building up others to love and trust God. We are all here, and each day we have a purpose. Every day we are presented with an opportunity to share Christ. I just pray that we will be awake to it, see it, be open to it, and act when called. If we are not sure of our foundation, we can easily be swayed and thus not available to share Him with those around us because we are not rooted in what we believe. What we believe is rooted in whose we are.

We are fully God's, but my question is this: Do we build our lives and truly live out of the place of being securely built on Him? This is not confidence; this instead is absolute dependence on Him. We must choose to set each day on God, laying our false strength and false plans for the day at His feet. We must also build on God because He knows where to leave room. If we plan our day without His insight, we can put the emphasis on where He wants us to pull back. We can fill and miss opportunities because we made ourselves too busy and too rushed to see them.

We must believe and embody this and not just say that everything happens for a reason. God ordains everything. Even if you feel as though you have learned the lesson and things need not persist, He is still persistent. He wants you to cling to Him. So if that means you are stuck at an airport for 24 hours, you are dealing with a sick loved one, or you are confused with where your life is going, that is exactly where God wants you. Sometimes He lets us stay in spaces or lets us constantly build on things we feel as though we have already learned it for just one person we are to meet later. Sometimes we think we are learning lessons so we can impact a multitude of people, but it could be for just one person. All of heaven rejoices when just one sinner is converted and enters the Kingdom of heaven rejoicing in their secured eternity. Luke 15:7 says, "Just so, I tell you, there will be more joy in heaven over one sinner who repents than over ninety-nine righteous persons who need no repentance." Do not waste what God is teaching you. You never know when or who will need it.

Build your life on God. It may take stone by stone, mortar by mortar, pillar by pillar, but it will be worth it. Your life was given to you by Him. It is built on His story and sustained by His grace, and it will be fulfilled by His glory and power. One step at a time, one moment at a time, and every breath in, through, and to him—let's get building His Kingdom.

References

Alcequiez, Elvis. "Can Willows Trees Damage Foundations? (Solved)." *Forever Architect.* September 6, 2021. https://foreverarchitect.com/can-willows-trees-damage-foundations-solved/.

Bajpai, Pratima. "Colloid and Surface Chemistry." In *Biermann's Handbook of Pulp and Paper: Paper and Board Making.* Amsterdam, Netherlands: Elsevier, 2018.

"Basement Waterproofing." *SAS Services.* February 20, 2023. https://sasbasementwaterproofing.com/.

"Building on Rock: Why It's Critical to Get the Foundation Right." *J. B. Simmons.* https://www.jbsimmons.com/blog/building-on-rock-get-the-foundation-right.

Department of Civil Engineering, Addis Ababa University, Faculty of Technology. "CEng 487 - Soil Mechanics II." https://smartaau.files.wordpress.com/2014/03/chapter1.pdf.

"Different Soils & How They Affect Foundations." *Ram Jack.* August 31, 2015. https://www.ramjack.com/about/news-events/2015/august/different-soils-how-they-affect-foundations/.

Edens, David. "10 Tips for Maintaining a Healthy Home Foundation." *Edens Structural Solutions.* February 15, 2023. https://edensstructural.com/maintaining-healthy-home-foundation/.

Edens, David. "Cracks in Walls or Foundations: Which Ones Are Structural Problems?" *Edens Structural Solutions.* February 15, 2023. https://edensstructural.com/cracks-in-walls-or-foundations-which-ones-are-structural-problems.

Emadi, Samuel. "Theological Triage and the Doctrine of Creation." *The Gospel Coalition.* October 20, 2015. https://www.thegospelcoalition.org/article/theological-triage-and-the-doctrine-of-creation/.

Foley, Nora K. "Environmental Characteristics of Clays and Clay Mineral Deposits." *U.S. Geological Survey.* Last revised April 1, 2009. https://pubs.usgs.gov/info/clays/.

"Foundation: Differential Settlements." *Geotech.* https://www.geotech.hr/en/differential-settlements/.

"Genealogy Chart from Noah to the 12 Patriarchs." *Conforming to Jesus Ministry.* https://www.conformingtojesus.com/charts-maps/en/noah_to_12_patriarchs_chart.htm.

Kibbel, William. "Stone Foundations – Cause for Concern?" *Old House Web.* https://www.oldhouseweb.com/how-to-advice/stone-foundations-cause-for-concern.shtml.

Lindsey, Joel. "When Jesus Hurried." *The Gospel Coalition.* July 2, 2015. https://www.thegospelcoalition.org/article/when-jesus-hurried/.

Obinna, Ubani. "Differential Settlement of Foundations." *Structville.* April 24, 2022. https://structville.com/2022/04/differential-settlement-of-foundations.html.

"Rocks and the Rock Cycle." *Paradisevalley.edu.* https://www2.paradisevalley.edu/~douglass/v_trips/wxing/introduction_files/rocktypes.html.

"Selection of Foundations Based on Different Types of Soil." *The Constructor.* August 24, 2018. https://theconstructor.org/geotechnical/selection-foundation-based-different-soil-types/8414/.

Sumerall, Alexander. "Building a Stone Foundation." In *Build a Cob House,* 2014. https://www.thiscobhouse.com/building-a-stone-foundation/.

This Old House. "House Foundations: Types and Common Problems." *This Old House,* This Old House. https://www.thisoldhouse.com/foundations/21071846/house-foundations.

U.S. Department of Agriculture. "Foundation Preparation, Removal of Water, and Excavation." *Natural Resources*

Conservation Service. July 2012. https://directives.sc. egov.usda.gov/OpenNonWebContent.aspx?content= 32418.wba.

Valle, Giovanni. "Can You Build on Clay Soil?" *Your Own Architect.* November 22, 2020. https://www.yourown architect.com/can-you-build-on-clay-soil/.

Weil, Ray R., and Nyle C. Brady. *The Nature and Properties of Soils*, 15th Edition. Harlow, England: Pearson Education Limited, 2017.